KU-021-178

INSHORE NAVIGATION

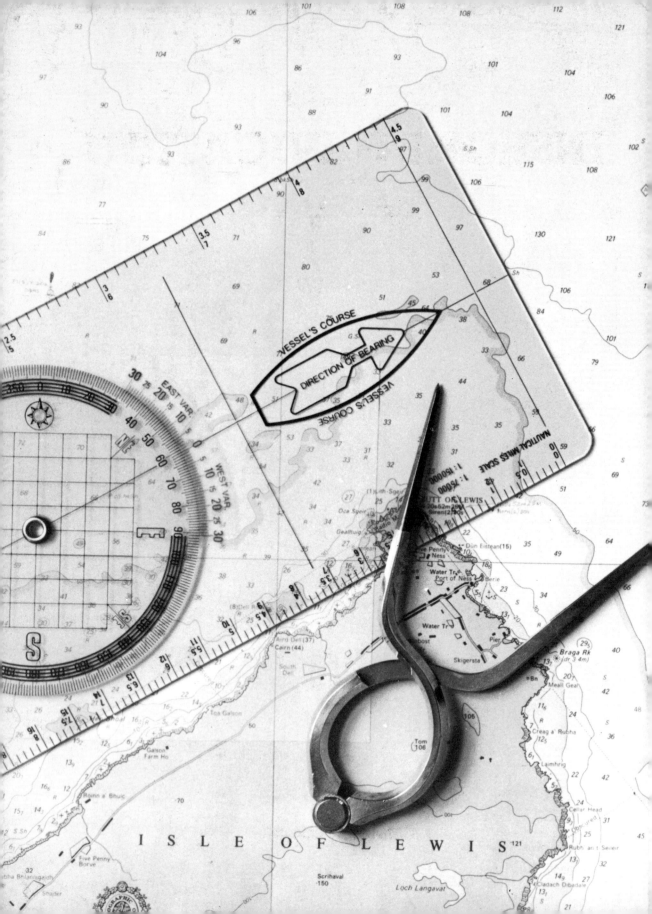

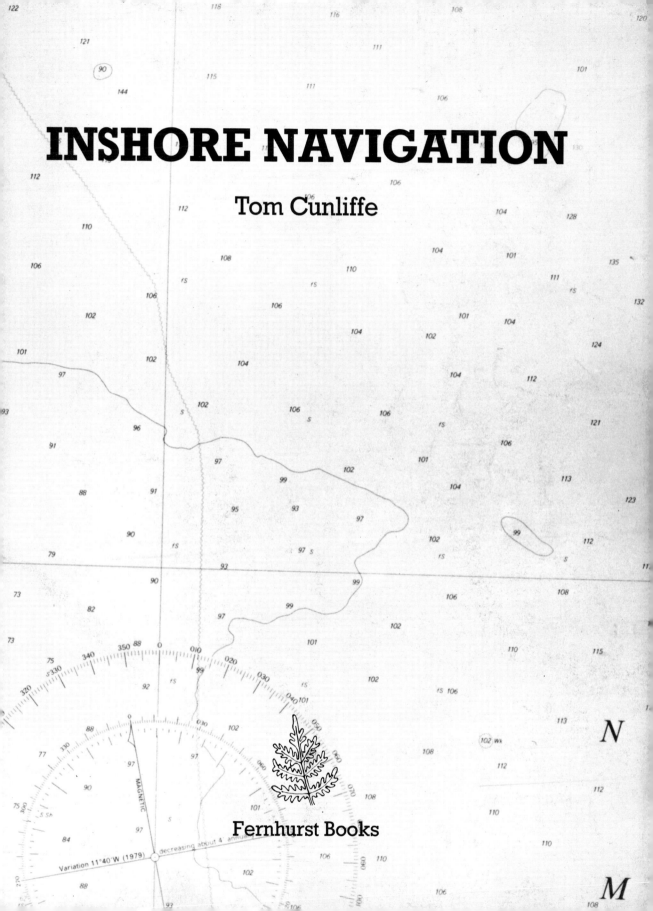

INSHORE NAVIGATION

Tom Cunliffe

Fernhurst Books

© Fernhurst Books 1987

First published 1987 by
Fernhurst Books, 31 Church Road, Hove, East Sussex BN3 2FY

All rights reserved. No part of this publication may be reproduced, stored in a retrieval system, or transmitted in any form or by any means, electronic, mechanical, photocopying, recording or otherwise, without the prior permission of the publisher.

ISBN 0 906754 31 3

Design and artwork by PanTek, Maidstone
Composition by A & G Phototypesetters, Knaphill
Printed by Ebenezer Baylis & Son Ltd, Worcester
Printed and bound in Great Britain

Contents

Acknowledgements

The author and publishers would like to thank Mike Best and the Westerly Sea School, Hamble, for the loan of a Westerly Fulmar, and Chris Wood of Yachtmail, Hamble Point, for the loan of navigational equipment for the photo sessions. Thanks are also due to Bill Anderson for his helpful comments on the manuscript.

The Admiralty charts and tidal information reproduced in this book are Crown Copyright, reproduced from Admiralty charts/publications with the permission of the Controller of Her Majesty's Stationery Office.

The portion of chart NZ 532 on page 42 is reproduced by permission of the Hydrographer RNZN.

Tidal information from the Macmillan & Silk Cut Nautical Almanac reproduced by permission of Macmillan Publishers Ltd.

Photographs

The photographs on pages 13, 31 and 53 are by Janet Harber. All other location photography by Tim Hore. Studio photography by John Woodward.

Introduction

The object of this book is to give a yachtsman enough knowledge to be able to navigate simply and safely on short inshore passages. The logical way to begin cruising is to make day sails in reasonable weather and steer clear of night passage-making until you have gained a little confidence. There is enough information here to enable you to do just that.

The book is structured so as to help you get on the water as soon as possible and stay out of trouble as you learn the necessities. All the essential navigational concepts are covered, so that when you feel your sea-going experience is sufficient you will be building on a solid foundation as you move into the greater depth of detail required for coastal and offshore navigation.

Navigation is not a text-book subject that flourishes in dusty classrooms. It is a living science that draws breath from the wide clean sea and the narrow tidal creeks. Once you have mastered a few simple principles you can only learn the art of its application in the great schoolhouse of the open water. Your best teacher is going to be yourself. Here are the rudiments. The rest is up to you.

Tom Cunliffe

1 Direction and the chart

Given that there is enough water to float your boat, navigation divides into two main sections. The first is being able to work out where you are and where to find your destination. The second is deciding how to move from one place to another.

In the simplest case of all, you can see your destination. There is no current and there are no intervening obstacles. All you have to do is to steer from one place to the other. This will hold good in still water over any moderate distance, but if your destination is too far away to be made out with any certainty, then in order to steer to it successfully you will need to use a *chart*.

Charts

Charts are published by the Admiralty and are available for all the waters you are likely to sail. They give sufficient detail for any normal navigational purpose.

A chart is a very detailed map produced to the highest standards of accuracy. It shows the coast, the foreshore and the sea with its depths and the nature of its bed. It also shows a variety of objects that will help you to work

Below: A line drawn on the chart from your present position to your destination represents the 'course to steer'. It is identified by a single arrow.

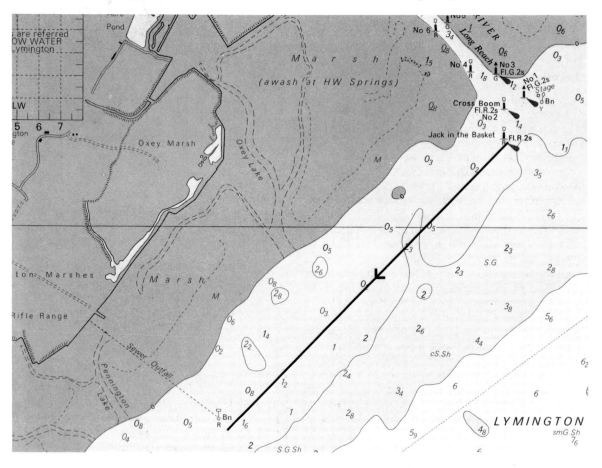

your way from one location to the next. Many of the symbols on charts are self-explanatory and some will be covered in this book, but if you are venturing out to sea you should have on board a copy of Admiralty publication 5011 which lists all the chart symbols. No-one can learn them all, but the best way to become familiar with the common ones is to get out on the water and to use your chart. They will soon become second nature.

Chart corrections

If you buy Admiralty charts from an official chart agency they will be corrected up to the date when you buy them. Every week the Admiralty publishes new corrections for world-wide charts in the *Admiralty Notices to Mariners*. Because there is far more information in these notices than will ever be required by yachtsmen and fishermen in home waters, the Admiralty now publishes less frequently a 'Small Craft Edition'. This gives all the information you will need and is available from a chart agent, or by post from the RYA if you prefer.

Correcting charts is satisfying work and to do it once in a while will not only give you up-to-date charts and some useful plotting practice, but will also keep you out of the pub for an evening.

Direction

In order to find out which way to steer towards an unseen destination, you first take your chart and with a *soft* pencil (which is easier to rub out) draw a neat line from where you are to where you want to go. Put one arrow on the line to show that it represents a *course to steer*.

Obviously you cannot draw a line on the sea to steer along, so you need some form of directional reference to link the line on the chart to the direction you are actually steering. This link is the *compass*.

If you look at the section of chart in the illustration you will see an example of a *compass rose*. This shows the orientation of the chart in degrees of a circle. Notice that there are two concentric roses. The outside one shows north (000° or 360°), pointing exactly to the top of the chart while the inside rose indicates it a little to the left, or west. The outside rose points to the geographic north pole and is thus indicating *true* north. The inside one points to the magnetic north pole which lies some distance from the geographic pole. This rose is indicating *magnetic* north, which if your boat's compass is accurate is where it will be pointing. The difference between true and magnetic north is called *Variation* and it changes between one area and another. For a given location, however, it is always to be found on the compass rose on your chart.

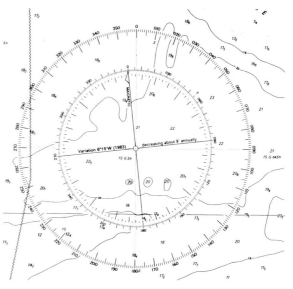

Above: The compass rose on a chart.

In order to determine the direction of the 'course line' you have drawn on the chart you will need to use an instrument to transfer it to a convenient compass rose. One way of doing this is to use *parallel rulers*.

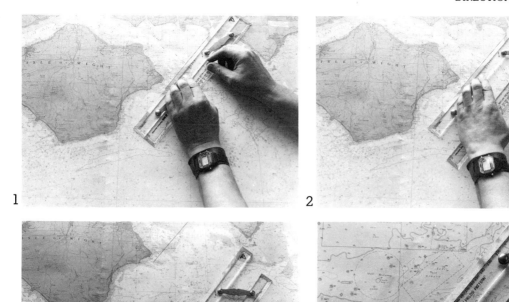

Above: Using parallel rules to find the bearings of a course line. The rules are laid along the line (1) and the section furthest from the line swung open (2). This is then held down while the other section is moved to close the rules. This is repeated until one edge of the rule bisects the compass rose (3, 4).

Courses and bearings are always expressed as degrees of a circle in a three-figure notation to avoid confusion, with noughts pronounced 'Oh'. It is important to get into the habit right from the start of noting whether a course is *True* or *Magnetic*.

Very often there will not be a convenient compass rose beside the course line, and if you are using parallel rulers you will need to 'walk' them across the chart. On the chart table of a small yacht, well heeled in a seaway, this is well nigh impossible and so most yachtsmen make use of one of the commercial brands of plotter instead.

One such device is the Breton Plotter. This has its own compass rose which can be aligned with the north-south grid lines on the chart while the course is read off at the pointer. Because there is a Variation scale which can be marked up for the present location, the course can be read off as either Magnetic or True, just as it can at the compass rose on the chart.

✠ True and Magnetic headings ✠

For centuries, the compass was divided into 32 *points* and all courses were given as north, east etc, or some sub-point in between. Wind directions are still forecast on the old system so it is as well to have it fixed clearly in your mind.

Nowadays people rarely refer to the points of the compass when giving a course because degrees of a circle are easier and more accurate to use.

Compass Variation, however, is still expressed as either 'east' or 'west' of north. What this means in practice is that if the Variation is 6° West, then the north pointer on the Magnetic rose will be 6° to the left of the north pointer on the True rose.

True north will be the same heading as 006° Magnetic, and magnetic north will be the same as 354° True.

Any compass heading will be greater than the true heading by the same amount.

So, if the Variation is to the west, the figure for the course Magnetic is *greater* than the figure for the course True.

If the Variation were given on the chart as being 5° East, the opposite would apply and the magnetic north pointer would lie 5° to the right of the true north pointer.

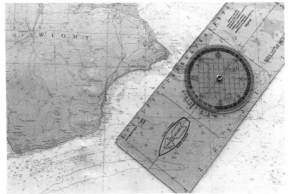

In this case, true north will be 355° Magnetic and magnetic north will be the same as 005° True.

Any compass heading will be less than the true heading by the same amount.

Thus if the Variation is to the east, then the figure for the course Magnetic is *less* than the figure for the course True.

Above: A Breton Plotter is simply laid along the course line; the grid on the central rose is aligned with that of the chart (left) and the bearing is read off against the mark indicating magnetic Variation.

Below: If the Variation is 6° West a course of 060° True will be 066° Magnetic; if the Variation is 5° East the same course will be 055° Magnetic.

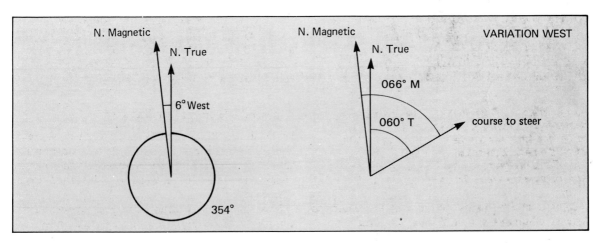

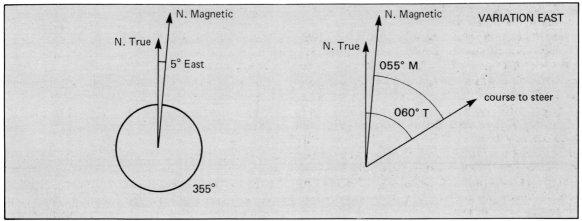

Sometimes courses, bearings, or leading lines into harbours are supplied on Admiralty charts. These are always expressed in degrees True, so although you may choose to do most of your plotting directly in Magnetic, it is important to be able to convert from one to the other when necessary. If you have time you could draw one of the little pictures shown above, but sometimes you need to be quicker than that and in those cases, most people enjoy the help of a mnemonic such as this:

ERROR WEST – COMPASS BEST (i.e. biggest)
ERROR EAST – COMPASS LEAST

If you have a leading line given at 045°T with 6° West

Below: By aligning two posts in transit a rower can stay on course despite a crosswind.

Variation, then: Error West, Compass Best. The compass course must be 6° *bigger* than the true course, so the course Magnetic would be 051°M. And, of course, the converse applies if you are converting from Magnetic to True.

It doesn't matter whether you plot in True or Magnetic. The choice is entirely up to you, but for goodness sake don't forget the 'T' or the 'M' suffix after each heading or bearing, because otherwise you'll forget which you have selected and the result will be total confusion.

✳ Leeway ✳

Any boat on a course with a cross-wind blowing is going

Below: The rower knows he has been blown off course by the way the transit opens (top picture).

to find itself pushed downwind of its destination. It's the same for a rowing boat crossing a lake or a powerful cruiser reaching along the coast, and the effect is called *leeway*. Leeway may appear to be insignificant, but if it is ignored a lot of grief and maybe some expensive navigational inaccuracies will be incurred.

If you are in sight of your destination it is easy to see if you are being blown sideways by lining up two objects so that one is behind the other when you are on track for your goal. If they *open* (i.e. move one against the other), then you are drifting from your direct line and you must steer in order to *close* them again. Two objects lined up and used in this way are called a *transit*. This technique forms a vital part of all practical pilotage.

You can see that the boat in the illustration is having to 'head up' about 10° in order to stay on the line. If he steers straight for his destination he drifts off course, the transit opens, and he has to steer firmly upwind of his course to close it up again.

If you cannot see your destination and are plotting a course, you will have to make an estimate of how much leeway to allow for. As a rule of thumb, a small sailing boat closehauled in a stiff breeze may make anything up to 10° leeway. On a reach its leeway will diminish steadily as the wind draws further aft until on a run it has disappeared completely.

Motor boats are also subject to leeway so if you are under power don't forget that it still exists!

Below: The rower over-corrects for leeway, and the transit opens the other way.

Below: By keeping the transit closed, correction for leeway is achieved automatically.

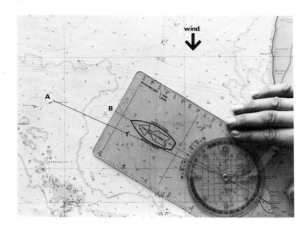

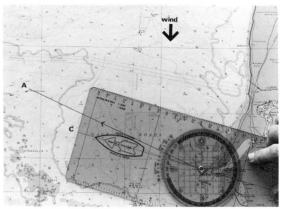

Above: Applying leeway. Starting from the 'course to steer' line (A) the plotter is turned into the wind to give a course made good (B).

Above: Turning the plotter away from the wind indicates your actual course (C) if leeway has not been applied to the course to steer.

It's easy to get muddled up when applying a leeway correction to a course to steer, and your chart can very soon start to look like a spider's web of pencil lines. The way to avoid this is simple. Place your plotter on the course to steer and lightly sketch a wind arrow somewhere on the chart. Now imagine your boat is sailing up the edge of the plotter and see which way you'll have to turn it to counteract her tendency to be blown downwind. Since you will be steering a little upwind, turn your plotter 5° or 10° towards the direction from which the wind is blowing and read off the heading. That is the course to steer.

If you have not applied leeway to your course and are wondering where on earth your real course line is taking you, you can apply the same technique. Sketch the wind arrow on the chart, place your plotter on the course steered, and then turn it 10° or so *away* from the wind. Now you know!

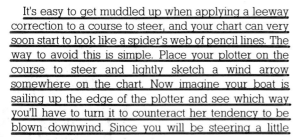

2 Distance and time

Chapter 1 dealt with the navigational dimension of direction. You know which course to steer to move the boat towards its destination, and you also know the direction you have followed from your point of departure. The other two important dimensions to the inshore navigator are those of *distance* and *time*, which are related to one another by *speed*.

A knowledge of *distance* together with *direction* is vital because these two form the basis from which you are able to work out where you are. *Time* is important because it provides a regularly changing navigational reference point, and *speed* is probably the most useful planning tool of all.

As on land, speed is expressed as the amount of distance travelled in one hour, so if you know how fast your boat is likely to be going, you know how far you can hope to travel in a day. On the other hand, if time is running short and you still have a known distance to travel, you can see how fast you must go to arrive within the time you have set.

Time is the same at sea as it is anywhere else on earth. It is a measure of the turning of the globe, and a glance at your wrist-watch will tell you how it is getting along.

Distance is measured in *nautical miles* which are about 2000 yards (1800 metres) long. Speed is measured in nautical miles per hour which are generally known as *knots*.

In the days before modern measuring instruments were invented, it was easier to observe speed through the water than distance run. Given speed and time, of course, distance could be readily calculated.

Speed was measured by using two instruments. One was a half-minute sand glass like a giant egg-timer, and the other was a free-spinning reel of rope with knots tied at regular intervals and a device on the end known as a log. The log was hove over the stern and the mate turned the glass as the first knot ran off the reel. The number of knots in the half minute gave the speed in nautical miles per hour.

Incidentally there were generally 17 knots on an optimistic clipper ship's reel, and on one infamous occasion the coolie holding it up was jerked over the stern as the last of the line whipped out before the half

minute was up. The captain came on deck to enquire as to the speed of the ship. 'Seventeen knots, and a Chinaman', retorted the mate, and went happily off watch.

Today, instruments for measuring distance run are still known as *logs*. Generally simple mileometers, many have a speedometer function as well.

Trailing log

This is a basic instrument measuring miles and tenths of a mile. It is extremely robust and functions by measuring the turns of a spinner towed astern on the end of a line known as the *log line*.

Below: A trailing log (top) and spinner (centre).
These logs have to be zeroed by hand: foolproof!

These instruments are very reliable, and the current matt black spinners do not attract fish; the older polished brass items acted rather like mackerel lures, and seemed particularly appetising to sharks.

The trailing electronic log

This works on the same principle as the mechanical trailing log and tows a spinner, but the log line is much shorter and is actually a length of electric cable which transmits a pulse generated by the turning of the spinner. The 'read-out' end can be mounted simply in the cockpit at the inboard end of the cable, or it may be mounted remotely at the chart table. This is also a reliable, inexpensive instrument.

The electronic impellor log

Impellor logs are a great convenience because they save all the trouble and potential problems (such as fouling the propellor) associated with log lines. They function by employing a tiny, rotating impellor mounted

Below: A trailing electronic log (top) and a
multifunction electronic readout.

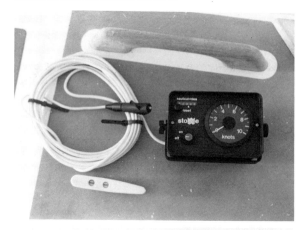

on the outside of a through-hull fitting which transmits its message to a remote display unit. The impellor can usually be drawn into the hull at sea. This is a very useful feature because it allows you to clear it of the tiny bits of weed which love to slow it down and upset its readings. These logs are beautifully made and last for years, but you pay for the convenience.

The global grid

Before discussing distance on charts, it is important to have an understanding of the *global grid* system.

This enables any point on the Earth's surface to be pinpointed with a two-dimensional reference. One set of lines runs north to south and is known as the *longitude* scale, while the *latitude* scale runs round the world from east to west.

Longitude

From the diagrams you can see that longitude is measured east and west from the *prime meridian* which passes through the Greenwich Observatory.

Since there are 360° in a circle and 180° in a half circle the lines of longitude, known as *Meridians*, spread out from Greenwich and meet at 180° East and 180° West on the other side of the world.

Each degree is divided into 60 minutes and each minute into tenths. Dover, for example, is at about 1°20' East, and Plymouth at 4°10' West.

Notice that because lines of longitude converge at the poles they are never the same distance apart from one degree of latitude to the next. Because of this they are not useful as a measurement of actual distance, but they do provide valuable and accurate reference points.

Latitude

To measure distance, we use the lines of *latitude*. Notice that unlike the meridians of longitude which cut the Earth like segments of an orange, the lines of latitude are all parallel and equidistant from one another. They are, in fact, known as *Parallels of latitude* and are measured north and south of the equator which is designated as 0°.

Southern England falls around the early fifties, with Harwich at about 52°N and Falmouth at a few minutes over 50°N. Kirkwall in the Orkneys is at 59°N and the Arctic Circle comes at around 67°N.

Right: The global grid system. The meridians of longitude (top) are measured east and west of the Prime Meridian (0°) at Greenwich. Parallels of latitude are measured north and south of the equator.

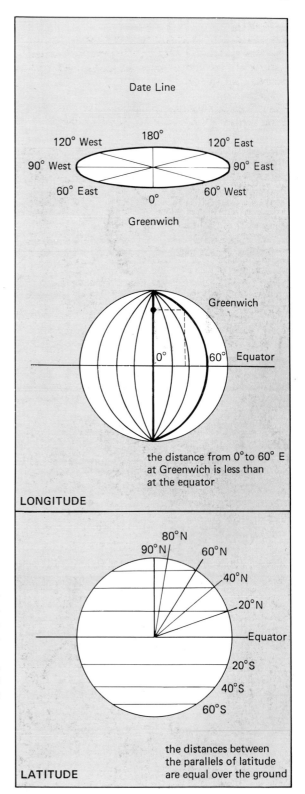

Above: Using single-handed dividers to measure the distance between two points on the chart.

Above: Transferring the dividers to the latitude scale gives the distance in nautical miles.

Like the meridians, the degrees of latitude are subdivided into 60 minutes and the minutes into tenths. It is a happy arrangement that *One minute of latitude* is equal to *One nautical mile*. This means that in order to see what the scale of a chart is you have only to look at the minutes of latitude to know what a mile looks like.

Whatever you do, *don't* use the longitude scale at the top and bottom of the chart to ascertain distance. It will work out perfectly on the equator, but the results grow more disappointing as you travel north and south. By the time you reach the Pole you will be able to stride from one degree to the next!

To determine the distance between two points on the chart you will need a pair of *dividers*. The pair being used in the illustrations are of the 'one handed' type, and are well worth the extra expense because you can hang on to your can of beer with one hand while manipulating your dividers with the other.

The charts you will be using for inshore navigation project the surface of the Earth onto the flat paper in one of two different ways. On some deep-water charts this affects the way the meridians are shown, but for all practical purposes you can consider the meridians of longitude on a coastwise chart to be parallel with one another. This is particularly important when you are using them as a grid against which to line up your plotter.

✳ The dead reckoning position ✳

Right from the start, *distance run* and *course steered* are the corner-stones of your navigation.

Suppose you are sailing along the coast from a harbour to a river mouth. The river mouth may prove difficult to

Below: Checking a Dead Reckoning position using observation of an object marked on the chart.

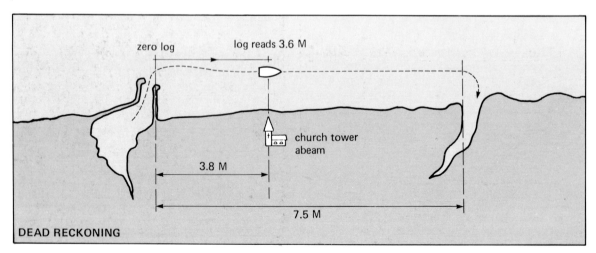

zero log

log reads 3.6 M

church tower
abeam

3.8 M

7.5 M

DEAD RECKONING

spot, so the only way you know its whereabouts is by measuring its distance from the harbour entrance on the chart and comparing that with the distance shown on your log. If there is no current or tide, when the two coincide you should be there, or thereabouts.

A position worked out from course steered and distance run is called a *Dead Reckoning position* (DR) and is marked by a small vertical cross on the chart.

If you are sailing along the same stretch of coast as in the previous example and you decide to check on how you are getting on, the first thing to do would be to put a DR position on the chart and note the time beside it. Inspection of this shows that abeam of this position on the shore is a church tower. Have a look and see if it is there. If it is, then you have some good evidence that all is well. If it is not, you had better find out what else has been affecting your progress.

This is an example of one of the most fundamental principles of all: *Always use what you can see to check whether you are where you think you are.*

✳ The log book ✳

Since time does not stand still, and distance in a vessel under way is always moving on, the navigator is constantly referring back to known or estimated positions. He needs to do this in order to work up his current whereabouts, or make projections as to his future movements. For this reason all positions, observations and significant events must be systematically set down in a *log book*.

Any exercise book will do for this function. A hard back is better in the long run but it is the contents that

Below: How to lay out a log book, using hand-ruled columns in an exercise book.

count rather than what is inscribed on the cover.

Starting with the blank page, the illustration shows how it should be ruled off into columns. Simplicity is the watchword. The simpler the entries, the more inclined you will be to make them when you are wet, cold and maybe seasick as well.

Everything that may be of navigational interest is *logged*. There's no need to write an essay in the events column, but get enough down to ensure that you'll understand it a few hours on.

The columns shown here are sufficient in most cases, though some people like to put an extra column in for estimated leeway. If you find you are getting confused by leeway then use a column to remind you what's happening to it. Otherwise, remember, the simpler the better.

To see how vital a log is, consider this example:

Time	Log	Course	Weather	Event
1400	32.6	245M	Fair S2/3	Gasworks Creek entrance
1430	35.2	245M	"	Green buoy close to port

As you can see from the diagram the buoy could be one of two, but the DR position at 2.6 miles on a heading of 245M from Gasworks Creek entrance places you very close to one and well way from the other. In all probability, that is the buoy you are close by.

Note that a visible and recognisable object is being used again to check up on your DR position. Without the log book there would be no DR, so keep it up to date. Your life may depend on it.

Below: Identifying the buoy is easy if all the course details are entered in the log book (see text).

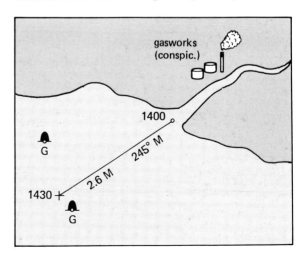

3 Buoys and beacons

Buoys, beacons, lighthouses and all the other man-made aids to navigation are the nearest things to signposts that the sea has to offer. Like a signpost on the road a particular buoy may be a vital part of your journey, or it may be virtually irrelevant. It's important to be able to recognise the different types at a glance, so that you can make up your mind as to which is which.

Along with the rest of Europe, Great Britain has adopted the International buoyage (IALA) system 'A' which means that the shapes, colours and positions of buoys and beacons are not haphazard. They are arranged according to a scheme which is so clear that, once understood and memorised, it will go a long way to keeping you out of trouble in rivers, estuaries and coastal waters, even if your chart has blown over the side.

Lateral marks

These are generally used to indicate either boundary of a well-defined navigable channel. To decide which side is which, the important thing to ascertain is the *direction of buoyage*.

Where a channel is leading towards, or further up a harbour or estuary, the red markers will be on your port side and green to starboard when you are travelling from seaward.

If the markers are numbered, you'll find that they number upwards from the seaward end of the channel, with the odd numbers to starboard and even numbers to port.

In open water you will occasionally come across lateral markers which do not lead to any particular port. In these instances, the direction of buoyage is 'clockwise' round continental land masses. For this reason, in British waters, if you are heading from south-west towards the north-east, the reds will be to port and the greens to starboard.

In theory a green starboard-hand buoy is a conical shape, and its red port-hand counterpart is 'can' shaped, with parallel sides. In practice, particularly with some of the larger main channel buoys which may be of steel lattice-work construction, the shape is not all that clear. Sometimes, such a buoy will carry a topmark ('cone' or 'can') to tidy up any ambiguity, but in some cases you have to rely on the colour and the suggestion of a shape.

Any starboard-hand marker that is not a buoy (it will usually be a green post driven into the seabed and may be called a *beacon*) will carry a similar triangular

Below: Lateral marks entering an estuary: red cans to port, green cones to starboard.

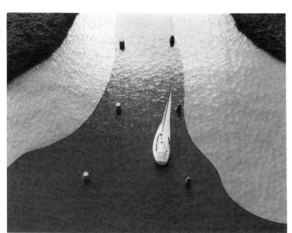

Below: A conical green starboard-hand buoy, and (inset) as it appears on the chart.

Above: A large 'conical' starboard-hand buoy.
Below: A large port-hand 'can' buoy.

Above: A lit port-hand pile, complete with a tide-gauge which is indicated on the chart.

topmark. Port-hand red posts will, of course, carry a square, can-shaped topmark.

The photographs show a variety of lateral markers ranging from the highly professional Trinity House-serviced, lit navigational buoy to beautifully painted baked-bean tin perched on top of a withy. For a yacht both may be equally effective.

If a port-hand marker carries a light, it will be red, and will flash with a rhythm which will be described on the chart. Lit starboard markers carry a green flashing light.

On the chart
Lateral buoys appear on the chart as mini buoy-shaped symbols, conical or can-shaped. On the lower edge of the buoy is a tiny circle. This represents its true position. The colour is indicated by R (red) or G (green). If they have a name or number, as many do, this will be shown as well on the more detailed large-scale charts. If the mark is lit, it will have a magenta, lozenge-shaped 'flash' beside it, and its light characteristic will be described.

Above: Withies marking a channel, with a port-hand 'can' and starboard-hand 'cone'.
Left: A lit starboard-hand pile in a river mouth.

Beacons are shown by a ∗ symbol and their lights are similarly described. If they are unlit, they are shown simply as a small ∘ with the topmark indicated.

Cardinal marks

Where there is a hazard to navigation such as a rock or sandbank which isn't bypassed by a buoyed channel it may be marked by one or more *Cardinal* markers.

Cardinal marks are so called because the position of each of the four types relates to one of the four Cardinal points of the compass: north, south, east and west. Like lateral marks they are either buoys or beacons.

The buoy standing to the north of the danger is known as a North Cardinal buoy. It is easily recognised at close range in the daytime by its topmark, which consists of two 'north-pointing' cones. The topmark of the South Cardinal buoy points 'southwards' and also very easy to understand.

If you imagine the topmark of the West Cardinal laid on its side thus: ▶◀ it is not difficult to see the letter W as the lower half of the symbol. If this doesn't grab you, try

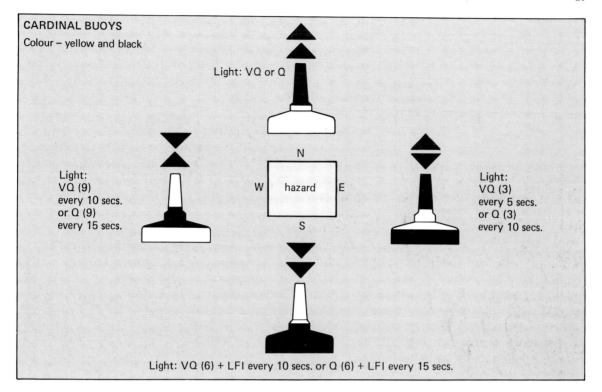

CARDINAL BUOYS
Colour – yellow and black

Light: VQ or Q

N

W hazard E

S

Light:
VQ (9)
every 10 secs.
or Q (9)
every 15 secs.

Light:
VQ (3)
every 5 secs.
or Q (3)
every 10 secs.

Light: VQ (6) + LFl every 10 secs. or Q (6) + LFl every 15 secs.

Above: The Cardinal buoyage system, showing the topmarks, colour patterns and light characteristics. Right: A typical South Cardinal buoy.

seeing the topmark as a bobbin, which it resembles after a fashion, and simply remember that West Winds Wool (WWW) Alternatively, think of the mark as Wasp Waisted.

The East Cardinal topmark ⬥ is so like the letter ∈ (E) in a thousand classical inscriptions that it needs no further elaboration.

At longer range these marks and buoys can be readily distinguished by the arrangement of their yellow and black colour scheme.

You'll notice that the North Cardinal is black at the top and yellow at the bottom. The 'pointers' of the topmark is indicating where the black is to be found. The South Cardinal topmark is pointing to the bottom of the marker, which is therefore black, and the top yellow.

The West Cardinal bobbin has its points indicating the middle of the marker, and so the central section is black, with the upper and lower parts picked out in yellow. Finally the East Cardinal topmark points to the top *and* bottom, so in this case they are both black with the yellow stripe in the middle.

You'll also notice that whoever worked out this

beautiful system carried his genius through into the way the marks are lit. If you imagine the diagram with a clockface superimposed upon it, you'll see that East is at 3 o'clock, South at 6, West at 9 and North at 12. The lights are all white.

The East Cardinal flashes 3 times (VQ[3] or Q[3])†. The South Cardinal flashes 6 times, with an extra 'long flash' to minimise confusion (VQ[6] + LFl).

The West Cardinal flashes 9 times (VQ[9] or Q[9]), and the North Cardinal flashes continually, 12 being rather a lot of flashes to count as you bounce along from wave top to wave top (VQ or Q).

If you come across a Cardinal marker you have not identified on the chart, just remember that it stands on its own side of the danger. To be sure of being safe, you should therefore pass to the north of a North Cardinal, and so on with all the other types.

On the chart

Cardinal buoys are usually of the 'pillar' type and they appear so on the chart. They are labelled BY (Black and Yellow), and the topmark is always shown so that you know what to look for. As with all buoys the name, if any, and light characteristics are shown beside it.

Safe water marks

Red and white buoys are often used to indicate the beginning of a buoyed channel and are then known as 'land-fall' buoys. They indicate the existence of safe water and can thus be left on either hand. If they are lit they show a white light which may be *isophase**, *occulting***, or one long flash every 10 seconds. Mid-channel buoys have single topmarks like some lateral buoys, only in their case the topmarks are spherical.

On the chart they are shown as miniatures of themselves with their name, light characteristics and the letters RW to indicate their colour.

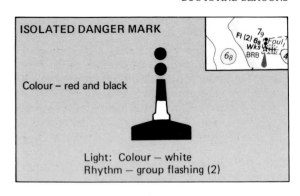

ISOLATED DANGER MARK

Colour – red and black

Light: Colour — white
Rhythm — group flashing (2)

Isolated danger marks

These marks, buoys or beacons indicate the position of a specific danger to navigation such as a wreck or a pinnacle rock, on top of which they are theoretically placed. Navigable water lies on all sides. It is a good idea to give these marks plenty of clearance as you will probably be unaware of the actual extent of the isolated danger. Their light characteristics are always Group Flash 2.***

Like Cardinal marks, isolated danger marks have a double topmark: two round balls, one above the other.

On the chart such a mark is indicated as a miniature buoy or beacon, showing its '2 balls' topmark, its light characteristics and the letters BRB to denote its colours: Black, Red and Black.

---

† Q is a chart symbol and means Quick Flash – one flash per second. VQ is Very Quick Flash – two flashes per second.
* Isophase (Iso) is a light whose characteristic is to show equal phases of dark and light
** An Occulting light (Occ) is 'on' most of the time, but 'blinks' off. Sometimes called a 'black flash'!
*** A light described as Group Flashing gives the stated number of flashes followed by a period of darkness to make up its time period. When the period is up it repeats its flashes, and so on.

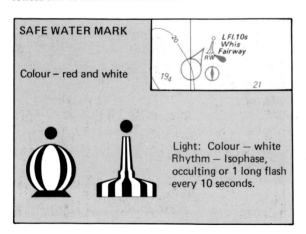

SAFE WATER MARK

Colour – red and white

Light: Colour — white
Rhythm — Isophase, occulting or 1 long flash every 10 seconds.

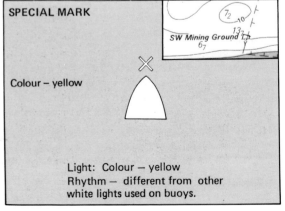

SPECIAL MARK

Colour – yellow

Light: Colour — yellow
Rhythm — different from other white lights used on buoys.

Special marks

Anything which needs marking that does not fall into one of the other categories is buoyed with a yellow *special mark*. These are used for all sorts of purposes including military exercise areas and water ski zones.

If they have a topmark it is always an 'X' and their lights, where fitted, are yellow. The buoys, themselves, may be any shape at all. On the chart the buoy is indicated by the usual miniature buoy showing its topmark, if there is one, its light if necessary, and the letter 'Y' to denote its colour.

Like all the other markers, its actual position is to be found by using the tiny circle on its base line.

A word of warning

While the position of buoys is accurately charted you should remember that they are not truly *fixed objects*, being only moored to the seabed. They can be a short distance away from their charted position, particularly in areas of extreme tidal activity, and it is not unknown for them to break loose and go off station altogether.

Lighthouses

Lighthouses are nothing more than large, sophisticated navigation beacons. They are intended primarily for night navigation, but many of them are magnificent, prominent structures, and make excellent day marks.

On the chart

Lighthouses appear as ★ symbols with the usual magenta flash denoting a lit aid to navigation. Beside the symbol is a statement of the light characteristic, with its

Below and right: Lighthouses range in size from classic round towers to the lattice-work structures often found on the ends of piers. The chart gives all the information needed for accurate identification.

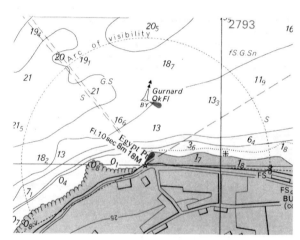

range in nautical miles (denoted by capital M), and the height of the structure in metres (denoted by a small m).

If you need further information as to what a lighthouse actually looks like, you will find a description in the passage notes of the proprietary nautical almanacs, or in the Admiralty *List of Lights*.

Making use of navigational aids

The first thing to understand about navigational aids once you know what they all mean, is that they are only put there to *assist* your navigation. You don't have to do what they suggest.

For example, if you are manoeuvring up a shallow creek with a foot of water under your keel and mud all around, you are going to be very well advised to stay within the channel marked by the piles and withies. On the other hand, if you are approaching a busy commercial harbour with a buoyed entrance channel, but plenty of water for your boat outside that channel, then you could well be better off if you stay clear of it. You may be able to cut off a corner by doing so, and also you will be out of the way of any large vessels steaming up and down between the buoys.

Similarly, a Cardinal mark may have been set up to assist the passage of supertankers, and the shoal which it marks may have enough water over it to float the *Cutty Sark*. If that is so, then its only relevance to you is as a useful position indicator. Check up on the chart and find out, but if in doubt, treat every marked shoal as a potential wrecker.

It's good practice to get into the habit of identifying on the chart each buoy you see when you are out sailing, whether you are specifically looking for it or not. That way you will learn to identify buoys rapidly and naturally. As with everything else, the more effort you put into your seafaring, the more competent you will become and the more you will get from your recreation.

Navigational aids must be approached with the same relaxed common sense as everything else at sea. Know them, understand them. Without them we are lost, in every sense of the phrase, but just because a buoy is green, it doesn't necessarily mean you have to leave it to starboard.*

---

* At sea, if you are going to pass an object on your starboard side, you are said to be leaving it to starboard.
The same thing applies to objects left to port.

Above: In a shallow tidal creek the withies often mark the limits of navigable water, and the yachtsman ignores them at his peril.

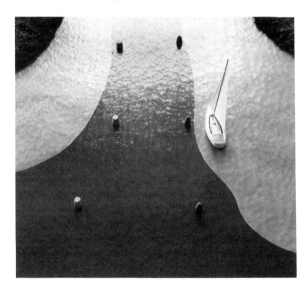

Above: The lateral markers of a deep shipping channel can often be ignored safely by a small yacht – but check the chart first.

4 Pilotage

While navigation might be described as the art of moving effectively from one location to the next and knowing where you are on the way, *pilotage* is the negotiation of the intricacies of the narrow waters at either end of the passage, or at any stage en route when there is neither the time nor the room to indulge in the broader techniques of open water navigation.

If you are setting out across a wide estuary with the other shore only dimly visible, you will be quite correct to work out a course to steer and then go off in that direction, but it is a mistake to think that if your safe route into a tricky river entrance takes you between two rocks you can miss them both by merely steering the necessary course from some distant point.

A helming error of a degree or two or a slight inaccuracy in the compass could be enough to plant you firmly 'on the bricks'. Furthermore, while predictions as to the strength and direction of tidal streams (see chapter 5) are available for the waters around the coast, in a pilotage situation the information is rarely of sufficient accuracy to rely on implicitly.

For these reasons, when you are piloting your boat in narrow waters, you need to make use of a few visual techniques to make sure that you are going where you think you are. First, we'll take a look at some of the methods you can employ and then we'll consider how to employ them.

The chart

The first thing to do is to study the largest-scale chart you have carefully, so as to familiarise yourself with the passage and orientate yourself as to its most important features. You'll be looking for enough water to float in, for the most direct and simple route, and for the necessary land and sea marks, by reference to which you'll know what is going on.

Depth of water

As in all boat movements you need enough water for your draught plus a suitable margin of safety which can vary a lot depending on the nature of the bottom and whether the tide is rising or falling. If you are in doubt about your ability to work out the tidal height (see chapter 8), you can always start off by using the charted depths of water, safe in the knowledge that there will

Below: A river entrance, showing the charted depths and drying heights of the banks and channel.

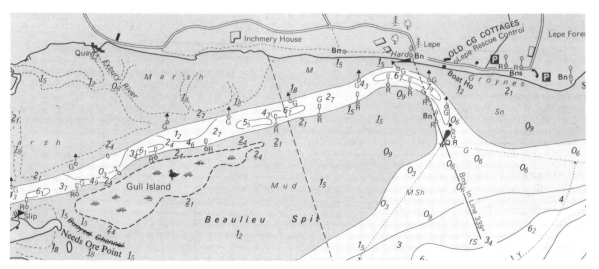

never be less than that. The unattached figures you see all over the chart are known as 'soundings'. They give the depth of water at that point in *metres*, and tenths of metres, when the tide is as low as it will ever be. If the figure appears on a green part of the chart and has a line underneath it (thus 1_3), it means that at the lowest of low tides that area will be 1.3 metres *above* sea level. It is called a *drying height*.

As you become more experienced you will be able to make fuller use of the state of the tide to help you penetrate more deeply into creeks and harbours of the coast.

Pilot books

In theory the chart gives you all the information you need for satisfactory pilotage, but a little local knowledge goes a long way in assisting the cause. Yachtsmen's pilot books are usually written by experts who have spent years studying an area. They know the pitfalls and the easy ways to success. Very often a pilot book will give you a point-to-point plan for the negotiation of a difficult piece of water which, when used with the chart, gives you the best preparation you can have. But whether you are using a pilot book or not, you still need to understand some basic principles.

Range

It is very useful indeed at sea if you are able to tell at a glance how far you are from an object. At close quarters this is quite easy, but it becomes increasingly difficult as ranges increase.

Twenty-two yards is the length of a cricket pitch. Simple to judge if you have ever been a cricketer. One hundred yards is a football pitch, maybe two hundred yards is the length of your street. Two hundred yards is a useful measure because it is one tenth of a nautical mile. This distance was also the length of one of the massive rope anchor cables of the Nelsonian navy, and ever since it has been known as a *cable*. A cable is the usual subdivision of a mile on the latitude scale of a chart, and pilot books frequently refer to distance in terms of cables.

Above a cable's length, ranges become increasingly difficult to determine by eye. Always be suspicious of your judgements and leave a good margin for error, but take every opportunity to look carefully across known stretches of sea in order to develop your sense of distance.

Below: When using a hand-bearing compass to take a bearing on a fixed object, the reading stays the same whichever way the yacht steers.

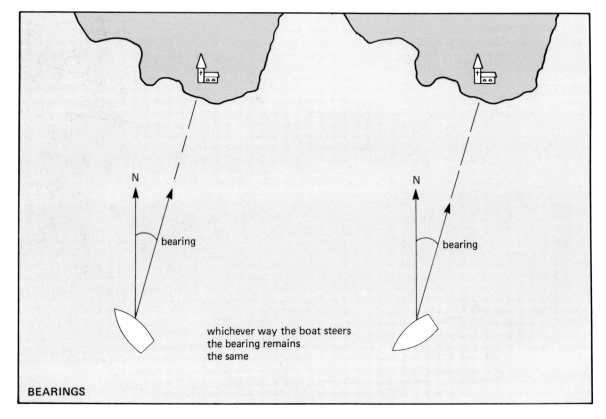

whichever way the boat steers
the bearing remains
the same

BEARINGS

✳ Bearings ✳

Just as a compass course to steer will take a boat from one place to another, a compass *bearing* will tell you the direction in which an object lies relative to your boat, or how your boat lies in relation to a fixed object.

If you are steering staight towards an object, your course will be the same as the bearing of the object, and you will be able to read it straight off your steering compass. If, however, the object is somewhere other

Above: Using a hand-bearing compass: the sights are aligned with the object and the bearing read off.

than directly ahead, you will need to use a *handbearing compass* to measure its bearing. These hand-held compasses come in a variety of forms with prices to match.

Below: The bearing transferred to the chart.

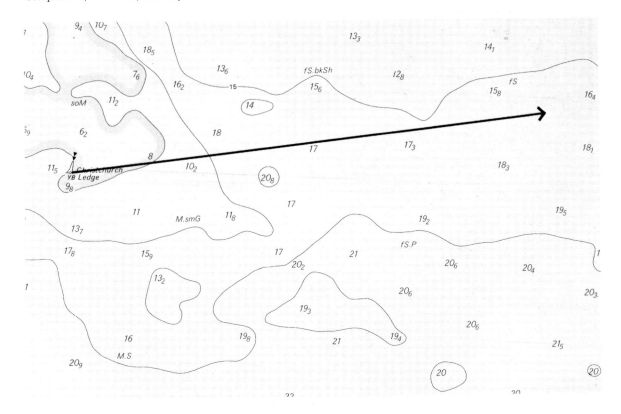

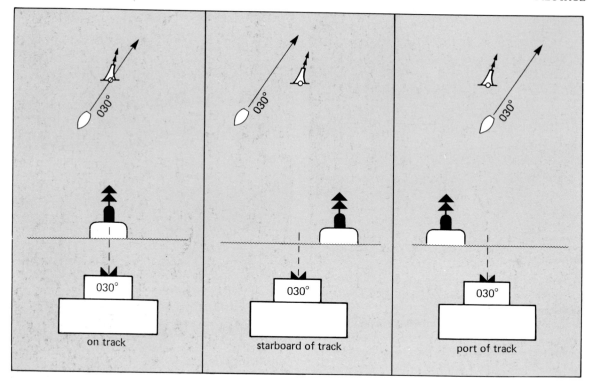

| on track | starboard of track | port of track |

Uses of bearings

Back bearings: If you know that in order to avoid a danger you need to stay on a particular line from a known departure point, or from a convenient, conspicuous object, you can keep on track by first determining what the bearing of the object will be as you sail away from it and then taking *back bearings* astern of you to ensure that the object continues to bear as it should. It is then a simple matter to make the necessary course corrections.

Clearing bearings: If you are approaching an invisible hazard with navigable water to one side of it, one way you can be sure of staying off it is by using a *clearing bearing*.

Figure 1 shows a yacht approaching a shoal. Beyond the shoal, and approximately in the direction the yacht is travelling is a dolphin (a structure of several posts joined together at the top, perhaps with a light on it). If you draw a line on the chart from the dolphin towards the yacht, passing just clear of the shoal, you have drawn a clearing bearing (Fig. 2).

In order to stay off the shoal the yacht must steer to the left of this line, keeping a check on the bearing of the dolphin. So long as the bearing stays at 320° or more, the yacht is clear of the shoal (Fig. 3). If the bearing becomes less than 320° (Fig. 4) then he is in dead trouble!

In this case, then, 320° is a *clearing bearing*. Notice

Above: Using a hand-bearing compass to stay on track using back bearings.
Right: Using clearing bearings (see text).

that when you are plotting its direction, you read from the boat to the object, because you will be on the boat, with your compass. To plot it the other way round would make it a *reciprocal bearing*, i.e. the actual bearing plus or minus 180°. This is an easy error to make.

✳Transits ✳

We have already seen the value of two objects in line when it comes to keeping a boat on track. When you become involved with pilotage, the *transit* really comes into its own. If you can ever substitute the transit of two objects ashore for a compass bearing you should do so, because a transit is totally unambiguous. Compasses swing about at sea and are sometimes difficult to read. They are subject to magnetic disturbance, and more than one staunch vessel has been put on the rocks by the steel rims of the navigator's spectacles! In a tight spot an error of two or three degrees can spell disaster.

In contrast a transit does not move. It is independent of the Earth's magnetic field, and as soon as the objects move apart by as much as a half degree, you can see you are off-line and make the necessary correction.

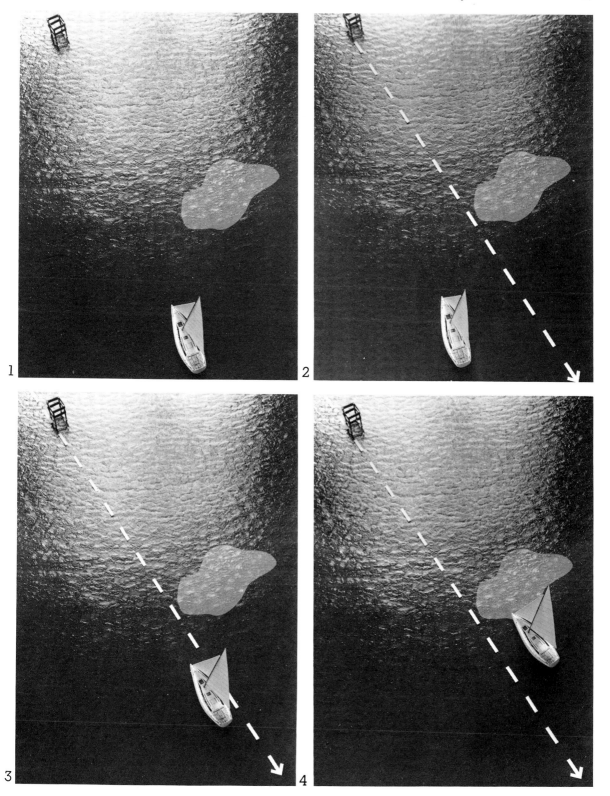

1

2

3

4

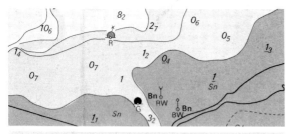

If no transits are supplied for you, you can usually manage to find some of your own, by careful inspection of the chart. For example, you might line up a buoy and a headland, or a church tower with the end of a pier. Of these two, the tower and the pier would be preferable as anything involving a buoy may be (very rarely) slightly less accurate.

Above and top: A permanent transit marking the deepest passage over a river bar; the rear post should be aligned with the V of the front post.

Above: Contriving your own transit: while the edge of the tower is aligned with the end of the breakwater the yacht will stay clear of the shoal.

If there is a cross-tide of doubtful strength and direction, a compass heading alone is almost useless, and a clearing or back bearing will need very careful watching. A transit is instant, it is visual and the helmsman can react to it straight away.

For this reason, safe leading lines for many harbour entrances are marked by permanently erected transits. For example, the markers shown in the photograph lead in over the deepest part of the bar of this river.

The worst case you will find is where you cannot come up with any suitable transit by perusing the chart. If the best you can do is to say, 'Well, I'll just have to head for that buoy on a course of 030M', what you must do is this: as soon as you leave your last mark and alter course to 030M with the buoy ahead, you line up the buoy with any discernable stationary feature of the background. Perhaps a fold in the hills will present itself, or maybe a solitary tree, or even a cow chewing the cud, so long as it

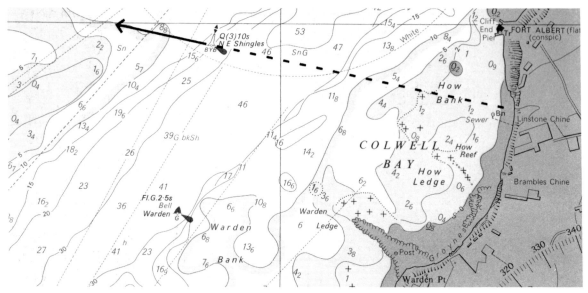

stays still! Then, even though there is no transit on the chart, you have come up with a *natural transit* which will keep you on your desired track, no matter what the tide or wind may do, until you safely reach the buoy, or your next course alteration.

You should always be on the look-out for ways of finding a bearing or a safe course to steer without using your compass. For example, it will be easy to draw a line on the chart to denote the point at which one island 'opens' from another (see illustration), or at the point where two headlands come into transit. It may be that just such a line will give you the route you need to thread your way through the shoals.

Above and top: Use of a natural transit: having got on track, stay there by aligning the buoy dead ahead with a fixed object – in this case a V-shaped mark on the shoreline – and keep it there.

The pilotage plan

Having now considered some of the possibilities available to the navigator when he turns pilot, you will realise that a pilot who is not properly prepared is a pilot who is likely to come unstuck.

It is not enough simply to come barrelling along towards an intricate stretch of water hoping that you will

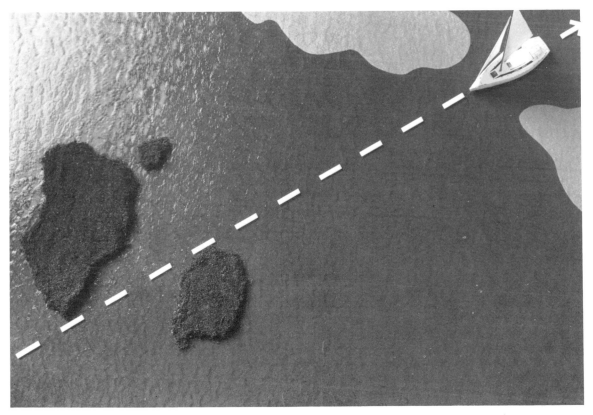

Above: In this case a transit taken between two islands ensures safe passage through shoal water.

be able to 'think on your feet'. You will need to be well prepared and, in all but the simplest situations, this means you are going to need a *pilotage plan*.

How you set about making up a pilotage plan is up to you, but it is best to make some good, clear notes on a pad or slate, and to mark up courses, distances and course alterations on the chart to correspond. When the pressure is on you will not have time to be fumbling around with your plotter; you will need to know right away. Incidentally, since crispness is of the essence when piloting, it pays to lay off all courses and bearings in Magnetic. That way you remove a common source of error, particularly popular with navigators under load.

In practice, as you alter course from one mark to the next you may find the new one difficult to identify if it is some distance away. The best technique here is to know how it should bear from your pilotage plan, and to place the boat straight away on the 'correct' heading. All hands then look for the mark ahead. As soon as it has been spotted you should line it up against its background, and keep it stationary as you proceed towards it. So long as you have picked up the mark in reasonable time, this will ensure that you stay on the safe track and are not set sideways. If in doubt, you can always take a back bearing on the mark you have just left. If all is well it will be on the reciprocal of the safe track to the next mark.

Should all else fail, and you feel yourself getting lost, don't be afraid to *stop*. It doesn't cost anything to anchor or simply slow right down while you 'get your bearings' and either is far better than plunging on hoping for the best but about to receive the benefit of the worst.

In a long channel with buoys or posts that are not numbered, it pays to tick them off on the chart as you pass them, otherwise it is all too easy to end up with one too many or one too few!

While all this is going on, the person in charge is usually busy taking bearings, spotting marks, lining up transits and the rest, so it is a great idea to put someone else on the helm. If you are properly prepared, you'll be surprised at how smoothly it all goes.

5 Tidal streams

Around the shores of the British Isles the tide can rise and fall anything from 4 to 45 feet (1.5–14 metres) twice a day. With that much water on the move it follows that tide-induced currents, known as *streams*, will be of great significance to the navigator.

In fact, tidal streams along the coast quite commonly run at 2 to 3 knots and in many places streams can exceed 5 knots. They tend to run up and down along the shore and so are usually either *with* you or *against* you.

If there is anything that is more important than the weather to the sailor, it is a knowledge of what the tide is doing. The average 28 foot (8.5 metre) sailing yacht cruises comfortably on a reach at 5½ knots. Suppose she is sailing into a *foul* tide of 3 knots her net speed *over the ground* is going to be 5½ minus 3, or 2½ knots.

If her prudent skipper has arranged to sail with *fair* tide the net speed of his yacht is 5½ plus 3, or 8½ knots over the ground. 8½ miles made good in one hour, as against 2½!

If that is not dramatic enough, the devastating effect of tide does not stop there. If our average yacht is now beating to windward, *distance made good through the water* in one hour after her tacks will be something like 3 miles.

In a foul tide, therefore, he is sailing on the spot. He has made good 3 miles in one hour through a patch of water which has, in the same hour, moved backwards the same distance. 3 minus 3 equals 0! In contrast the yachtsman sailing a similar boat to windward in a fair tide makes good 3 plus 3, or 6 miles in the same time.

Below: The effect of tidal streams. Sailing with the tide, the yacht covers over three times that achieved by a yacht sailing against the tide.

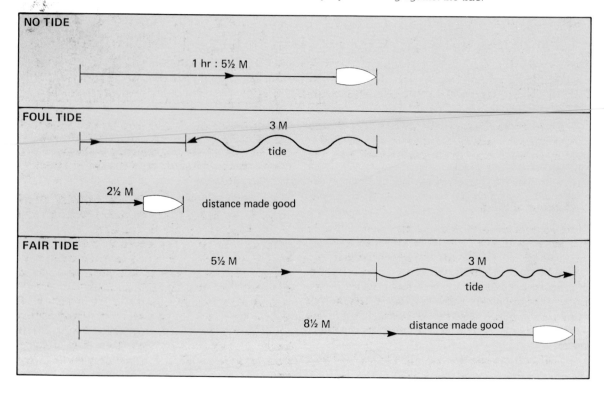

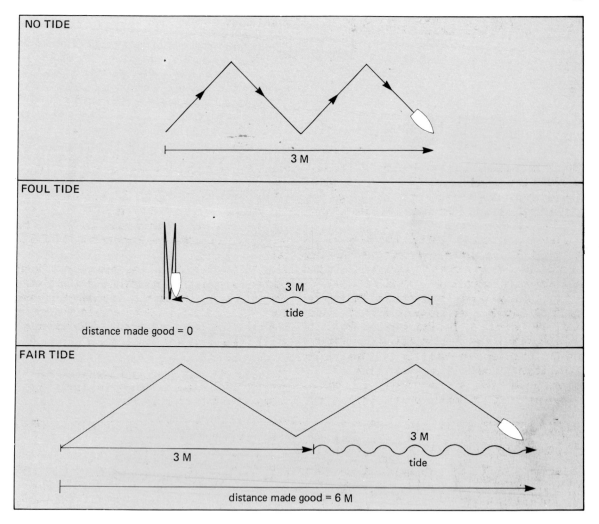

It should by now be as clear as crystal that, before setting out on any passage along the coast, you need to predict the times when the tidal stream will be going your way.

Above: A yacht attempting to beat upwind against the tide will get nowhere, but tacking with the tide increases the efficiency of each tack and may double the distance made good through the water.

The cause of tides

Tides occur because the waters which cover the sea are subject to the gravitational pull of the moon and, to a lesser extent, the sun. In mid-ocean these effects are not noticeable (and until recently not measurable either) but in the narrow waters around our shores the tidal surge piles the water up into some spectacular heaps. As it runs up the blind alley of the Bristol Channel, for example, it results in a tide that can rise up to 50 feet (15.2 metres).

At full moon and new moon the gravitational effects of the sun and moon act more or less in one line, so both bodies pull together and there is a large tide. At half moon, either waxing or waning, their effects act across one another, so the tide is much smaller.

These large tides are known as *springs* and the smaller ones, *neaps*. A spring tide generally moves twice as much water as a neap, and you will have already noticed that the word 'spring' has nothing to do with the seasons of the year. There are two springs each month, and two neaps as well. The tides generally stay at spring *High Water* levels, with correspondingly low *Low Water* levels, for two or three days. Then they moderate steadily to the much less extreme neap levels a week later.

APRIL

	TIME	m		TIME	m
1 TU	0331 0846 1611 2119	4.2 1.2 4.0 1.5	**16** W	0205 0822 1543 2052	3.8 1.6 3.7 1.9
2 W	0432 0956 1732 2247	3.9 1.5 3.7 1.9	**17** TH	0356 0921 1648 2209	3.6 1.8 3.5 2.1
3 TH	0559 1135 1915	3.6 1.7 3.7	**18** F	0510 1045 1817 2343	3.4 1.9 3.5 2.0
4 F	0030 0736 1309 2036	1.8 3.6 1.5 3.9	**19** SA	0641 1214 1937	3.4 1.8 3.7
5 SA	0149 0849 1413 2131	1.6 3.8 1.2 4.1	**20** SU	0100 0755 1321 2035	1.8 3.7 1.4 4.0
6 SU	0243 0940 1501 2213	1.3 4.1 0.9 4.4	**21** M	0154 0849 1411 2122	1.4 4.0 1.0 4.3
7 M	0323 1021 1540 2250	1.0 4.3 0.7 4.5	**22** TU	0237 0935 1456 2204	1.1 4.3 0.7 4.6
8 TU	0359 1057 1616 2323	0.8 4.4 0.6 4.6	**23** W	0319 1018 1540 2245	0.8 4.6 0.5 4.8
9 W ●	0433 1133 1651 2355	0.7 4.5 0.6 4.6	**24** TH ○	0400 1101 1625 2328	0.6 4.8 0.4 4.9
10 TH	0506 1207 1724	0.7 4.5 0.6	**25** F	0442 1146 1709	0.4 4.8 0.4
11 F	0028 0537 1243 1755	4.6 0.7 4.5 0.7	**26** SA	0011 0526 1233 1751	5.0 0.3 4.8 0.5
12 SA	0059 0608 1318 1824	4.5 0.7 4.4 0.9	**27** SU	0054 0610 1321 1833	4.9 0.4 4.7 0.7
13 SU	0128 0637 1351 1850	4.4 0.8 4.3 1.1	**28** M	0137 0654 1411 1916	4.7 0.6 4.5 1.0
14 M	0157 0707 1423 1921	4.3 1.0 4.1 1.4	**29** TU	0223 0742 1504 2007	4.5 0.9 4.3 1.3
15 TU	0228 0740 1459 1959	4.1 1.3 3.9 1.7	**30** W	0315 0838 1607 2113	4.2 1.2 4.1 1.7

Tide tables

The times and heights of high and low water for a series of major ports are published each year. These ports are known as *standard ports* and the information given about their tides in the tables is vital to working out your local tidal streams.

Illustrated are the tides for April 1986 at Portsmouth. By simply inspecting the heights of tide on various days you can tell which are spring tides and which are neaps. On the 26th, High Water achieved 5.0 metres. That is the highest tide and is clearly a spring. But on the previous weekend, the 19th, High Water was a puny 3.4 metres. A gentle neap.

Rivers

Tidal movements in rivers are easy to predict. The tide *floods* up river between Low Water and High Water. It *stands* for a while at High Water and then *ebbs* towards the sea until Low Water, after which the cycle is repeated.

In a tidal river, the ebb is generally stronger than the flood because as the tide rises it holds back the natural tendency of the river to flow towards its mouth and the 'fresh' water backs up. Once the ebb is established the river can revert to doing what rivers are supposed to do and the whole lot runs out in a hurry. In the Conwy river in North Wales, for example, it is not unusual for a spring ebb at the height of its power to be running at a full 7 knots.

Tidal streams along the coast

Along the coast the tide breathes in and out with the same regular rhythm as it does in the rivers, but the timing and direction of its changing movements are not always so easy to predict.

Tidal stream atlas

To enable you to see at a glance what is happening and what is going to happen, you should make use of a *tidal stream atlas*.

These are published by the Admiralty in a big, easy-to-read size, but they are reprinted in an acceptable form in the various commercial almanacs. Each page of the book refers to one hour of the full 12-hour tidal cycle, and is given a reference as so many hours *before* or *after* High Water at the relevant Standard Port.

The illustration shows a page from the Isle of Wight Tidal Streams Atlas. Notice that the page is designated 2 hours

Left: The tides for April 1986 at Portsmouth, as depicted in the tide tables.
Right: A page from a tidal stream atlas.

CAUTION:— Due to the very strong rates of the tidal streams in some of the areas covered by this Atlas, many eddies may occur. Where possible some indication of these eddies has been included. In many areas there is either insufficient information or the eddies are unstable.

2 **BEFORE**
HW PORTSMOUTH

1h 45m before HW
DOVER

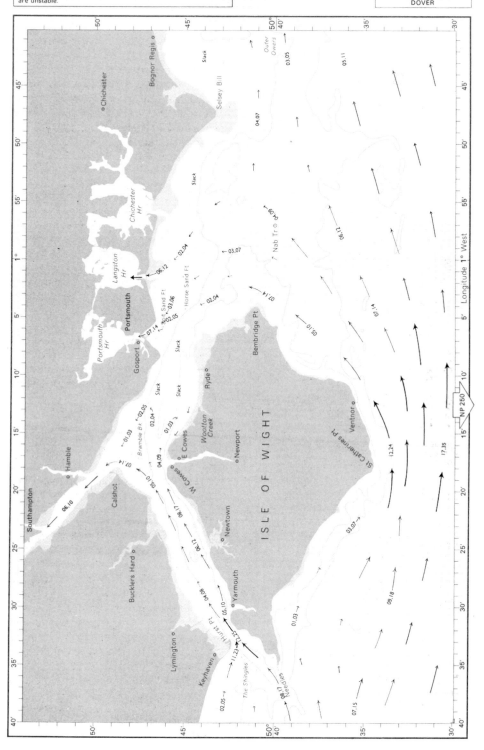

before High Water Portsmouth. It is almost self-explanatory except that the speeds of the tide given seem rather extreme. This is because the decimal point is missed out for the sake of clarity. Thus, the stream off the south point of the Island is not 12 24, it is really 1.2, 2.4. The 1.2 is the *neap* rate in knots and the 2.4 refers to *springs*.

When the tides are halfway (or a third, or some other fraction) between springs and neaps you will have to interpolate between 1.2 and 2.4 to determine the speed of the tidal stream on that day. If you are any good at mental arithmetic, the simplest way to interpolate is in your head. If this doesn't come easily don't get bogged down with complicated sums: turn to the inside front cover of the Admiralty Tidal Stream Atlas. There you will find a well-explained table which gives you the most accurate way of interpolating without recourse to mathematics.

Notice that the Atlas tells you what that tide is doing at a particular time. In fact the rate and direction of the stream are varying constantly between that time and the next hourly 'spot' (i.e. the next page in the book) but it is convenient to assume that the tide continues to behave as shown for a whole hour, changing on the minute to the characteristics shown in the next hourly prediction.

Because the information is given for a specific moment, in this case 2 hours before High Water Portsmouth, the hour to which the page refers begins at 2½ hours before High Water and ends 1½ hours before High Water.

A favourite navigator's error is to work on the basis that '2 hours before High Water Portsmouth' is when that particular page begins.

Tidal diamonds

If you do not have a Tidal Stream Atlas (or its almanac equivalent) or if you want a very accurate prediction of the speed and direction of the tidal movement at a given place, you can use the symbols known as *Tidal diamonds*. These are found in various places on most charts.

If you look in one of the corners of the chart there will be a section devoted to tidal information. The material in each column was collected at the location of the relevant diamond on the chart and, if you happen to be in the vicinity of that diamond, this system gives you an accurate way of plotting the strength and direction of the stream.

Note that all tidal stream directions given in the 'diamond' information are in degrees True, and the hourly prediction refers to the *middle* of the period in question, just like the pages in the Tidal Stream Atlas. So '3 hours after High Water Portsmouth' begins at 2½ and ends 3½ hours after High Water.

If you are positioned midway between two or more diamonds you will need a cool head and an inspired guess to work out what is happening. For this reason the Tidal Streams Atlas is generally a better bet for inshore work. With its light and heavy arrows, it also shows you at a glance the whole tidal picture of the area.

Streams in deep and shallow water

However carefully you lay your plans there will be times when you must run against the tide. This may occur through a miscalculation, or it may be that to make passage to a river mouth with the tide, you have had to take the ebb along the coast, leaving you no alternative but to punch against it once you are inside the river itself.

When this happens you will need to 'get out of the worst of the tide', and you do this by staying in the shallowest water you can safely sail in. The full strength of a tidal stream always flows in the deep water, and it is considerably slacker in the shallow water by the shore.

In a river, therefore, if you find yourself sailing against the tide you need to stay close to the bank. At sea, if it is safe to do so, you will have to crawl 'along the beach'.

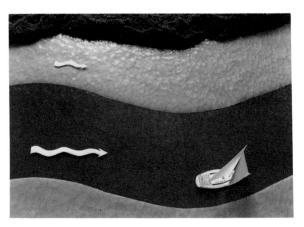

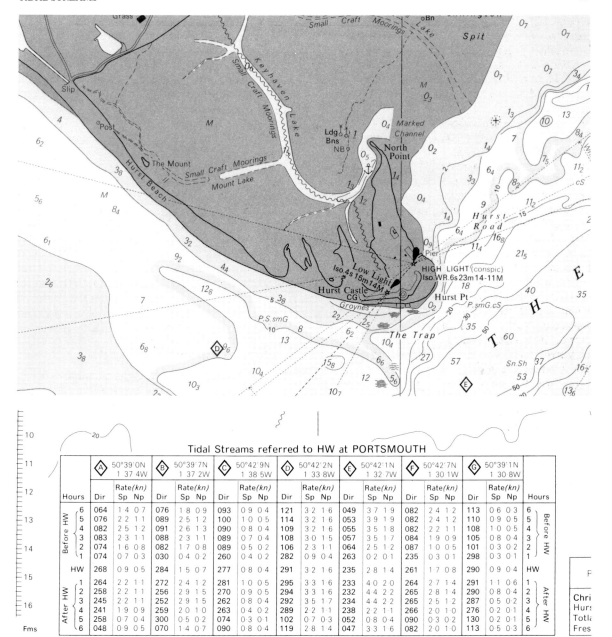

Tidal Streams referred to HW at PORTSMOUTH

	(A) 50°39'0N 1 37 4W			(B) 50°39'7N 1 37 2W			(C) 50°42'9N 1 38 5W			(D) 50°42'2N 1 33 8W			(E) 50°42'1N 1 32 7W			(F) 50°42'7N 1 30 1W			(G) 50°39'1N 1 30 8W			
Hours	Dir	Rate(kn) Sp	Np	Dir	Rate(kn) Sp	Np	Dir	Rate(kn) Sp	Np	Dir	Rate(kn) Sp	Np	Dir	Rate(kn) Sp	Np	Dir	Rate(kn) Sp	Np	Dir	Rate(kn) Sp	Np	Hours
Before HW 6	064	1 4	0 7	076	1 8	0 9	093	0 9	0 4	121	3 2	1 6	049	3 7	1 9	082	2 4	1 2	113	0 6	0 3	6 Before HW
5	076	2 2	1 1	089	2 5	1 2	100	1 0	0 5	114	3 2	1 6	053	3 9	1 9	082	2 4	1 2	110	0 9	0 5	5
4	082	2 5	1 2	091	2 6	1 3	090	0 8	0 4	109	3 2	1 6	055	3 5	1 8	082	2 2	1 1	108	1 0	0 5	4
3	083	2 3	1 1	088	2 3	1 1	089	0 7	0 4	108	3 0	1 5	057	3 5	1 7	084	1 9	0 9	105	0 8	0 4	3
2	074	1 6	0 8	082	1 7	0 8	089	0 5	0 2	106	2 3	1 1	064	2 5	1 2	087	1 0	0 5	101	0 3	0 2	2
1	074	0 7	0 3	030	0 4	0 2	260	0 4	0 2	282	0 9	0 4	263	0 2	0 1	235	0 3	0 1	298	0 3	0 1	1
HW	268	0 9	0 5	284	1 5	0 7	277	0 8	0 4	291	3 2	1 6	235	2 8	1 4	261	1 7	0 8	290	0 9	0 4	HW
After HW 1	264	2 2	1 1	272	2 4	1 2	281	1 0	0 5	295	3 3	1 6	233	4 0	2 0	264	2 7	1 4	291	1 1	0 6	1 After HW
2	258	2 2	1 1	256	2 9	1 5	270	0 9	0 5	294	3 3	1 6	232	4 4	2 2	265	2 8	1 4	290	0 8	0 4	2
3	245	2 2	1 1	252	2 9	1 5	262	0 8	0 4	292	3 5	1 7	234	4 4	2 2	265	2 5	1 2	287	0 5	0 2	3
4	241	1 9	0 9	259	2 0	1 0	263	0 4	0 2	289	2 2	1 1	238	2 2	1 1	266	2 0	1 0	276	0 2	0 1	4
5	258	0 7	0 4	300	0 5	0 2	074	0 3	0 1	102	0 7	0 3	052	0 8	0 4	090	0 3	0 2	130	0 2	0 1	5
6	048	0 9	0 5	070	1 4	0 7	090	0 8	0 4	119	2 8	1 4	047	3 3	1 6	082	2 0	1 0	113	0 5	0 3	6

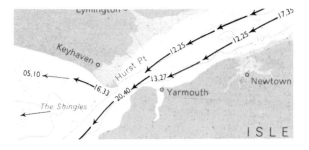

Top: A section of a chart showing a number of tidal diamonds, together with (above) the tidal information given on the same chart. This example is of a busy channel; normally the tidal diamonds are much more widely spaced. A section of the tidal stream atlas for the same area is shown for comparison (right).

Far left: Sailing close to the bank in a channel will enable you to make progress against the tide.

Left: If the tide is fair, make the most of it!

6 Estimated Position and the Fix

When you are on passage it is important to either know where you are, or to be able to work it out quickly with a minimum of fuss. The way you do this is work up an *Estimated Position* (EP) and then check it with a *Fix*.

In order to work up an EP you need to know first of all *where you started from*, or your *last known position*. For this information you will refer to your log-book.

The next thing to do is to put a DR position on the chart, corrected for leeway. It helps to draw in a 'course steered' line.

The last stage is to have a look in your Tidal Stream Atlas, or at the nearest tidal diamond to see what the tide has been up to. It's very helpful if you can arrange to plot your EPs to coincide with turning over a page in the Tidal Stream Atlas, because that way you have a nice, round hour's tide to plot.

You now place your plotter at the DR position and draw a *Tide Line* in the same direction as the relevant arrow in the Tidal Stream Atlas. The length of line will be the number of miles that corresponds to the estimated speed of the tidal stream in knots, if your EP is for a whole hour. If it is less than an hour, you simply make a 'pro rata' adjustment. Notice that the tide line carries three arrows.

At the end of the tide line you draw a little triangle. That is your EP. You should write the time against it and, of course, note it in your log book.

Just as a guide, plotting an EP should take seconds, rather than minutes. If, before you begin your passage

Below: Having drawn the 'course steered' line to the Dead Reckoning (DR) position, add the tide line to give an Estimated Position (EP).

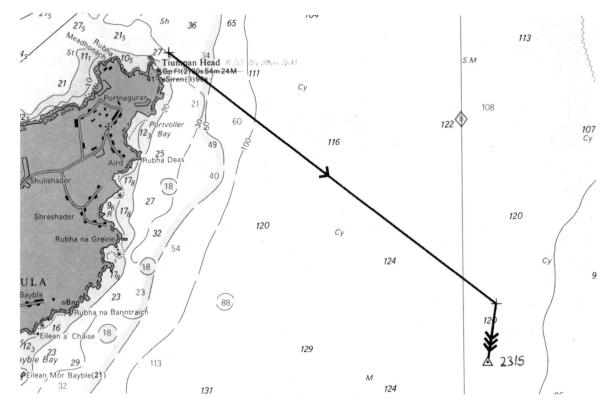

you note the time of High Water at the required standard port and decide if today's tides are springs, neaps or half-way, you will save a great deal of book-worming.

Here, once again, is what you do:

1 Find the course steered and distance run from your last known position (log book).

2 Place your plotter on the chart and alter the course steered angle to adjust for leeway.

3 Plot your adjusted DR.

4 Check the tide in the Tidal Stream Atlas or 'diamond' information.

5 Plot the tide line.

6 The end of the tide line is the EP. *Log it.*

You should not expect phenomenal accuracy from an EP. The name does not imply it, and you probably won't get it. There are too many unknown variables. The tidal information you have is only a prediction. Wind and weather may, and often do, affect the activity of the tides. Your steering compass might not be perfectly accurate. (Where did you leave that screwdriver? – see Chapter 10). Your helmsman could be misleading you with the best will in the world about the course steered, and your

Below: Compass bearings of fixed objects are marked on the chart as position lines; two PLs will give a neat fix, but three or four are preferable.

log is probably somewhat less than one hundred per cent accurate.

If an EP is all you have in the way of a position, then you should cherish it, but treat it with suspicion. Usually, however, there are ways of checking up on it. The most important way is with a *Fix*.

Fixing your position

The first thing to do to confirm your estimated position is to take a good look around you. You may well find that the buoy which your EP suggested was nearly a mile away is really only a cable off. You might even be about to hit it and you can't have a much better fix than that!

If, in fact, you are close by an easily recognisable object, refer to the chart and see if it ties in with your EP. If everything adds up, you need look no further. Log your position and enjoy your sailing for a while.

If you are not close enough to anything to consider your position fixed, then you must deduce where you are by using *position lines* (PLs).

A PL is a line drawn on the chart in an observed direction from a known object. A typical PL is the compass bearing of a lighthouse. If, using your handbearing compass, you take the bearing of a visible object which you can recognise on the chart, then you

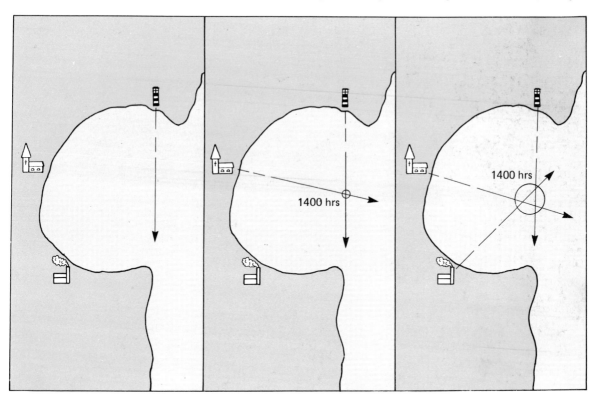

are somewhere on a line plotted on the chart along that bearing.

What you don't know yet is whereabouts on the line you are. In order to decide this you must find another PL (in this case a compass bearing on the church tower) and draw it in. Since you are somewhere on this PL as well as the first one, it follows that your position is at the point of intersection of the two lines.

If you can produce only two PLs, then put a neat circle around the intersection, label it with the time, and log it as a *Fix*.

In the illustration the faint lines leading from the lighthouse and the church towards the heavy PLs are only there to clarify the issue at this stage. When you are drawing PLs on your chart in practice, they should only be as long as they need to be to show the intersection, otherwise the chart rapidly begins to resemble the web of a non-union spider!

The three point fix

It isn't going to take much of an error in one of your PLs to place you a surprising distance from where you think you are. The classic counter for this possibility is the three-point fix. If you add a third PL to the fix you have an immediate check on its accuracy.

If the three lines coincide, or nearly so, then you have what is *probably* an accurate fix. Even so, you should still be cautious. Maybe for once the errors added up 'in your favour'!

If the lines do not coincide they will form what, for obvious reasons, is known as a *cocked hat*. The size and shape of your cocked hat gives you a good indication of the *area of position* in which your fix has placed you.

Below: A fix as marked on a chart; note that the position lines are restricted to the area of the fix itself, and not taken back to the bearing sources.

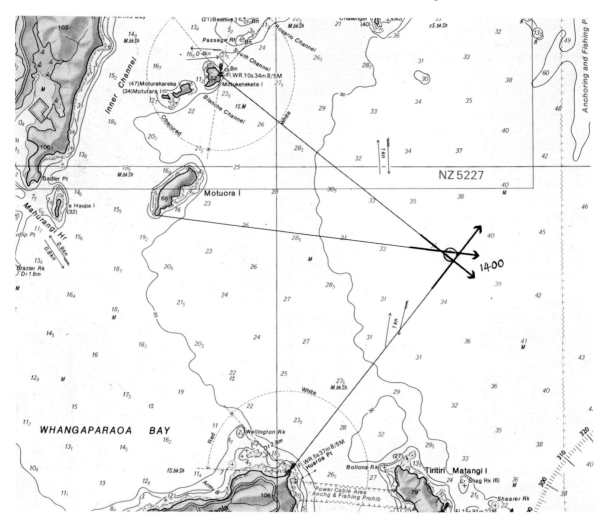

Obviously one or more of the lines is not quite accurate (or wildly adrift if the cocked hat is very large). You do not know which one, so the safest thing to do, if you have time and you don't like the size of your cocked hat, is to try again and see if you do any better. If the sea is rough it is quite likely that you won't improve on your first effort. In this case you must log the fix as it is, but *always assume the worst*. If part of your area of position lies closer than the rest to a danger, then proceed on the assumption that that is where you are.

Sometimes a fourth PL will help to clarify the situation by crossing neatly with two of the others, thus pointing the finger of suspicion at the third. You then have an idea of which of your PLs to check up on. *Don't* just throw the 'rogue' out. Maybe the fourth PL wasn't any good either!

Use of depth to check a fix or EP

The fix illustrated on page 42 gives the yacht's position as being in 36 metres of water. It makes sense, as you take your last bearing, to just flick on the echo sounder and note the depth. When the reading has been duly corrected for the height of tide (see Chapter 8), it should tie in with the depth marked on the chart. If it does not, then you should start asking questions.

The same technique can also be applied to an EP, and doing this is a habit well worth developing.

Logging fixes

A fix confirms (or otherwise) your estimated position by telling you where you were at a particular time. When you want to work up your next EP you will look back to that fix as a starting point for your course steered and distance run. It is, therefore, *vital* that you know what the log reading was *at the time of the fix*, not five minutes afterwards.

So take your PLs as quickly as you can and make a note of the log reading *before* you plot the fix on the chart. If often takes a beginner at least five minutes to do the plotting and if you haven't read the log, the fix is useless.

If you do forget to read it (and you wouldn't be the first) then be honest with your log book. Make a guess as to what the log should have read when you took your fix and enter that figure – *with a note of warning* alongside it. This is called 'cribbing the log'.

Sources of position lines

Whilst the compass bearing of a known shore object is a well-loved way of producing a PL, it is by no means the

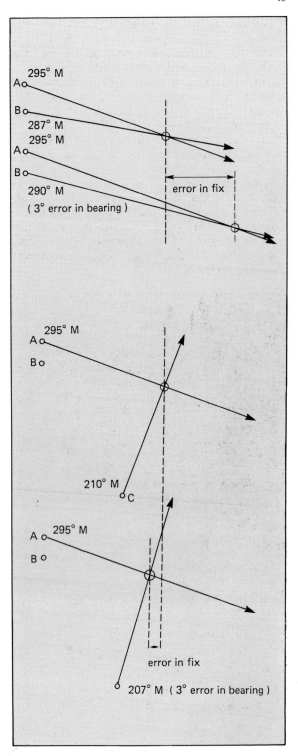

Above: A shallow angle of cut between PLs (top) will accentuate any error in bearings or plotting.

Sources of Position Lines	
Source	Quality
Compass bearing of a known object ashore or fixed navigational mark.	Generally good, depending on sea state.
Compass bearing of known buoy.	Fair, but the buoy may have drifted a little.
Compass bearing of the right-hand or left-hand edge of an island.	Generally good.
'Set up' shore transit.	Excellent.
Two known, clearly defined objects in transit.	Excellent.
Two less clearly defined objects in transit, e.g. two headlands lining up, or 'opening' on one another. (When one headland becomes visible from behind another as you approach, it is said to 'open').	Very good, except that it is not always easy to determine where a headland actually 'cuts the water'.
Bearing relative to the ship's head. Sometimes you need a quick bearing on an object and are not over-concerned about its pinpoint accuracy. If the object is nearly ahead or astern, simply steer in order to line it up with the fore and aft line of your boat and read off the steering compass. If it is abeam (sight down the mainsheet track or across the companionway to be sure) just add or subtract 90° from the ship's heading.	Fair. You can be very accurate if the object can be brought dead ahead. If it is abeam, you won't do quite so well.
Depth sounder.	Variable.

only one, nor is it necessarily the best. There are many other sources worth considering and some of these are evaluated above.

Planning fixes

A fix is only as good as its PLs and the angles between them. You should always try to make your PLs cross one another at a useful *angle of cut*. If the angle between two PLs is very small, it only takes a little error in one of them to lead to a large error in the fix. If the angle is good (60°-90° is ideal) a small error will not matter too much.

If you have a choice of two objects on roughly the same line which will give you the cut you want, always choose the *closer* of the two. An error of 2° in a bearing may be of little significance at half a mile, but at ten miles it can be devastating.

Sometimes you can produce a lovely fix using only two PLs by the technique of a *simultaneous fix*. A good example of this is a yacht steering a course with a known

Below: When taking bearings, the closer you are to the objects the better, as the effect of any bearing error increases with distance.

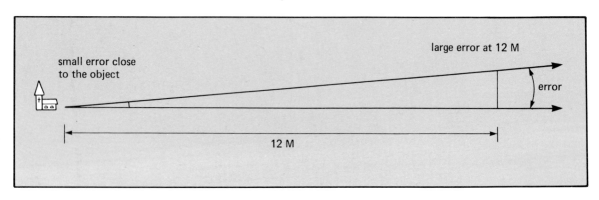

small error close to the object

large error at 12 M

error

12 M

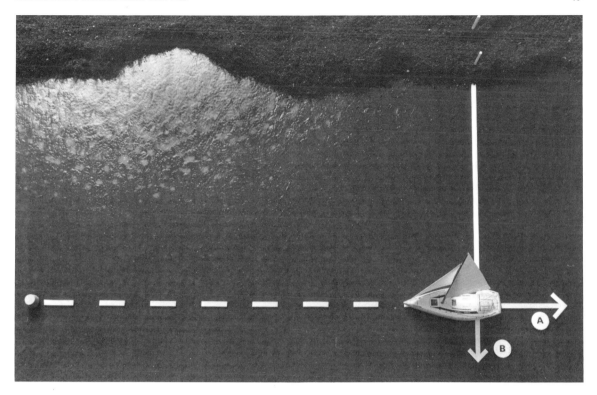

Above: Using the ship's heading (A) in combination with a beam transit (B) to get a simultaneous fix.

object almost ahead and a good transit coming up abeam. When the transit is almost 'on', you alter course to steer straight for the known object. At the moment the transit is made you note the ship's heading and the log reading. If your helmsman is steering a steady course, you have achieved a perfect fix of two excellent PLs, with a minimum of fuss.

Frequency of position updating

It is difficult to make hard and fast rules about how often a navigator should check and confirm his position. Much depends on circumstances but as a rule of thumb there should be a position on the chart at least every hour, at worst 'estimated', and preferably 'fixed'.

On some passages, and certainly as you approach your destination, this will not be enough. On the other hand, if you know a stretch of coast well, you may in time be able to navigate from one place to another in good visibility and put nothing on the chart at all.

A balance must be struck between the dangerously casual approach and the 'over navigation' of the inexperienced. Remember that you are travelling in a sailing vessel – not a classroom desk!

7 Course shaping

For many passages along the coast the tide will be running in line with your course, and will be simply fair or foul. But if you are crossing an estuary or sailing to an island you may well have to cope with a cross-tide.

This is done by making a suitable adjustment to the course to steer so that the boat slides 'crabwise' towards its destination. If your target is in plain view and you are able to transit it with something behind it, then this presents no problems.

The effect on the boat's heading when crossing a tide is clarified by the illustration, which shows a dinghy being rowed across a river with a strong tide running. Notice that the dinghy is 'pointing up' towards the tide although it is actually moving straight across the river. The rower is keeping an eye on the transits and compensating for the tide by visual inspection.

When you cannot see your destination, or are unsure of its whereabouts on a distant land mass, you need to work out how much to steer 'off' the direct track in order to achieve, on a larger scale, what the rower is managing when crossing the river.

The vector diagram

Because your tidal stream information is given in knots, it simplifies matters if you do all your calculations for periods of *one hour* or, rarely, exactly *half an hour*. As you will see, it is not necessary to try to work out exactly how long a cross-tide passage will take in order to deduce what course to steer.

This, step by step, is what you do:

1. Beginning at a known position 'A', draw in the *track* to 'D', your destination. The track line, or vector, is denoted by two arrow heads in the middle of it, thus:

2. Inspect the Tidal Stream Atlas to find what is happening to the tide and draw a line from 'A' in the

Below: A dinghy being rowed across a river in a cross-tide demonstrates how the track and tide vector are used to find the course steered.

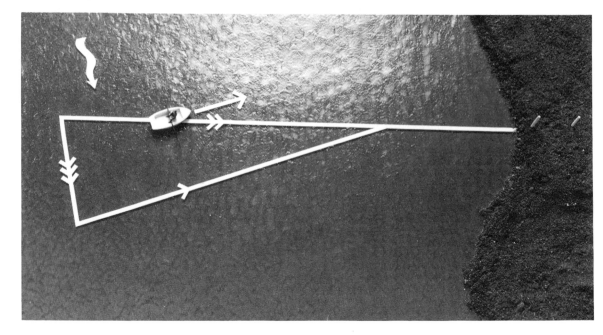

direction of the tide. The tide line, or vector, has three arrow heads, thus:

3. Take your dividers and, using the *latitude* scale of the chart set them for the predicted speed of the tidal stream in knots (i.e. miles per hour). Put one of the points of the dividers at 'A' and with the other scribe across the tide line, making a mark at 'B'. 'A-B' is now the completed tidal vector.

4. Using the latitude scale again, set the dividers at the number of miles you expect your boat to travel through the water in one hour. Then place one point at 'B' and scribe the other lightly across 'A-D' (the track) making a mark at 'C'.

5. Draw a line to join 'B' and 'C'. This is the actual course to steer and is given the symbol of one arrowhead:

6. All you have to do now is place your plotter on the course to steer, make any adjustments you want to make for leeway, and read off the required heading.

Note that the boat stays on the track line throughout the exercise and is doing exactly what the rowing boat did. It never goes near point 'B'. The whole construction is just a convenient pictorial means of working out how much you should lay off to compensate for the tidal stream.

The completed triangle is called a *vector diagram*. It is very rare for a vector diagram to be exactly the right size to take the boat perfectly from point 'A' to point 'D' but in practice this doesn't matter. The tide is unlikely to make any radical change in the last few minutes or so that it takes for the boat to traverse between 'C' and 'D'. Even if it does, by the time the hour is up your destination is usually well in sight.

If your point of arrival is obviously well within an hour's sailing, it is still easier to construct a full hour's vector diagram. Regardless of the physical size of the drawings on the chart, the boat will simply slide down the track until it reaches the vicinity of where you want to go.

Only if the scale of the chart renders a full hour's diagram a nonsense do you need to start dividing it up. Then, so long as you remember to halve the speed of the tidal stream and your own boat's speed, you will still achieve happy results.

A common mistake is to join up 'B' (the end of the tide vector) and 'D' (the destination). If this is done the diagram is rendered spurious because the 'course to steer' vector is too long and so represents the wrong speed for the boat.

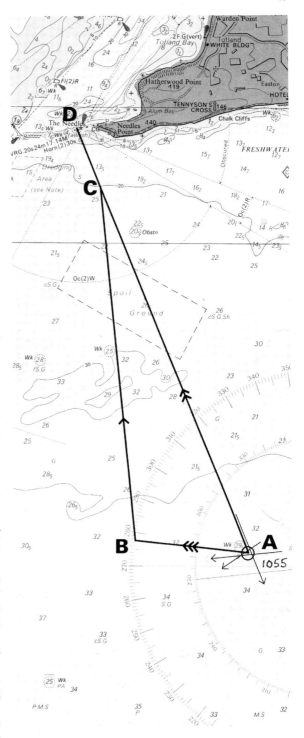

Above: A one-hour vector diagram drawn on the chart, using the arrow system to indicate the track, tide and course steered.

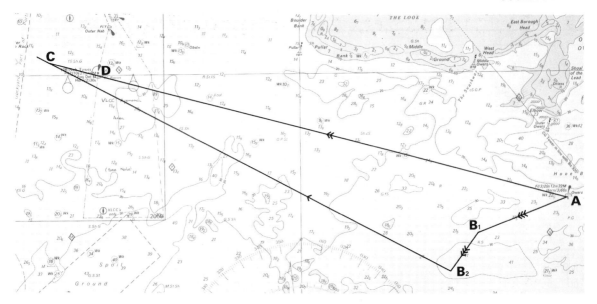

Above: A two-hour vector diagram on the chart.

If the passage across the tide looks as though it will take two hours, then draw two hours' worth of tide vectors out from 'A' and make 'B-C' (the course to steer time) two hours long.

Where 'A - B_1.' is the first hour's tide and 'B_1 - B_2 is the second, 'B_2 - C' represents the number of miles the boat is expected to travel in two hours.

If the tide vectors for the two hours are very different from one another, the boat may wander from the track during the period of the passage, but it should have returned to the track's vicinity by the end of the second hour.

Expectations of accuracy

We have discussed, in the chapter about Estimated Positions, the possible sources of error that may arise in calculations of this nature. You can hope for the best when setting up a course to steer but you must prepare for the worst. Often you will achieve results that will be highly satisfying, but from time to time all the errors will add up against you and you will end up considerably off track.

For this reason, it is important to study the proposed track carefully on the chart and, if there are any dangers close to it, make suitable modifications to your course in order to keep well clear.

8 Tidal heights and depth of water

We have already seen in Chapter 4 how depths of water are indicated on the chart by means of *soundings*. These are given in metres and tenths of a metre, and are quoted for a particular state of tide, known as Lowest Astronomical Tide (LAT). In theory at least this Chart Datum line is the level of the lowest Low Water that a really big spring tide can produce, so if your boat will float in the depth of water quoted on the chart, you are not going to run aground at that point due to a tidal miscalculation! (There are one or two exceptions to this rule. In a few rare cases, the height of Low Water in the tide tables will be indicated as a *negative* figure. When this happens, Low Water is actually *lower* than LAT and you will have to subtract its height from the soundings on the chart.)

Contour lines

In the illustration showing the chart of the Hamble River entrance, you will notice a number of *contour lines* separating areas of changing depth. By looking at the run of the contours you can get a good overall picture of the rate at which depths are altering.

Drying heights

Note that the depth inshore of the Warsash beacon is a *drying height*, expressed by a sounding with a line underneath. That little line will serve to remind you of two things:

- The sounding is sitting on top of the line, so at Lowest Astronomical Tide the 'depths' are above the level of the water by the amount indicated.
- In tidal height calculations the little line can be thought of as a minus sign, so when you are working out the actual depth of water, a charted drying height is to be subtracted from any extra water that the tide may be supplying.

Tide tables

In Chapter 5 you were using tide tables to see whether the tidal stream on a given day was going to be running at the spring rate, the neap rate, or at some rate between. You were also using the times of High and Low Water to determine when the tide would be ebbing or flooding.

Above: Part of a chart showing a river entrance.
Below: A section from A to B of the chart above.

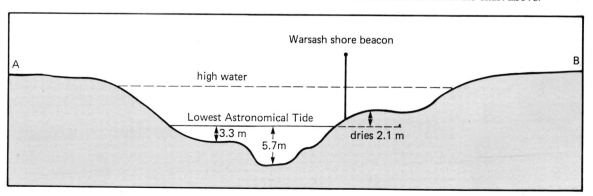

MARCH				
	TIME	M	TIME	M
1 SA	0242 0843 1504 2103	0.8 5.4 0.9 5.2	**16** SU	0245 0836 1459 2054
				1.3 5.0 1.5 4.9
2 SU	0321 0916 1544 2138	1.1 5.2 1.3 4.9	**17** M	0314 0908 1528 2130
				1.6 4.7 1.8 4.6
3 M	0404 0958 1629 2226	1.4 4.8 1.7 4.7	**18** TU	0349 0949 1604 2222
				1.9 4.3 2.1 4.3
4 TU	0457 1059 1729 2341	1.8 4.4 2.1 4.4	**19** W	0435 1052 1658 2339
				2.3 4.0 2.5 4.1

Above: March 1986 in the Plymouth tide tables.

Height of tide

Now you need to look a little more closely at what those figures of 'High' and 'Low' water actually represent. In fact, they show the *height of the tide* above the charted soundings at the times stated.

If, for example, a charted depth in Plymouth Sound is given as 5.3 metres and you want to know what the depth at that point will be at Low Water on the morning of March 3rd 1986, you inspect your tide tables and discover that the *height* of Low Water is 1.4 metres and that the time will be 0404 GMT.

The depth of water is going to be the
<table>
<tr><td>CHARTED DEPTH</td><td>5.3 m</td></tr>
<tr><td>plus the LOW WATER HEIGHT</td><td>1.4 m</td></tr>
<tr><td>=</td><td>6.7 m</td></tr>
</table>

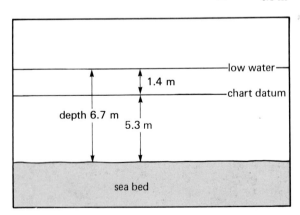

Above: Finding the depth of water (see text).

Similarly at High Water that morning, which comes at 0958 GMT, the depth will be the
<table>
<tr><td>CHARTED DEPTH</td><td>5.3 m</td></tr>
<tr><td>plus the HIGH WATER HEIGHT</td><td>4.8 m</td></tr>
<tr><td>=</td><td>10.1 m</td></tr>
</table>

British Summer Time

All times of tides given in the Almanac from British Ports are in Greenwich Mean Time (GMT). For this reason, during the period of British Summer Time it's necessary to *add one hour* to the time given.

Range of the tide

The difference between the 'High Water' and 'Low Water' figures for a given tide is known as the *range* of that tide. The range is the actual amount by which the tide rises and falls, and you will notice by inspection of the tide tables illustrated that ranges vary a lot between spring and neap tides.

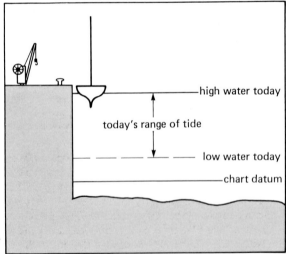

Above: Finding the range of tide.

Secondary Ports

Because there would not be enough pages in the almanacs to publish tide tables for all the ports around the coast, most of the smaller harbours are deemed to be *Secondary Ports* for the purposes of tidal information.

The times and heights of High and Low Water for each one are given by reference to the nearest Standard Port which shows similar tidal characteristics. These references are known as *Tidal Differences* and are expressed in various ways in the different almanacs.

SALCOMBE 10-1-17
Devon

CHARTS
Admiralty 28, 1634, 1613; Stanford 13; Imray C6, Y48; OS 202
TIDES
−0535 Dover; ML 3.1; Duration 0615; Zone 0 (GMT).

Standard Port DEVONPORT (◄─)

Times				Height (metres)			
HW		LW		MHWS	MHWN	MLWN	MLWS
0100	0600	0100	0600	5.5	4.4	2.2	0.8
1300	1800	1300	1800				

Differences SALCOMBE
  0000 + 0010 + 0005 − 0005 − 0.2   − 0.3   − 0.1   − 0.1
START POINT
+ 0005 + 0030 − 0005 + 0005 − 0.2   − 0.4   − 0.1   − 0.1

If you look at the tidal information for Salcombe, taken from McMillan's Almanac, the first thing to note is 'Standard Port DEVONPORT'. This means exactly what it says. The arrow points backwards to indicate that the tide tables for Devonport are to be found on an earlier page in the almanac.

Immediately beneath this, in the 'box' are four times of High Water and four times of Low Water. These refer to times at Devonport and they are all put in because the time difference between the two ports varies and depends on the time of High Water at Devonport.

If High Water is at one o'clock in the morning or one in the afternoon, for example, there is no difference at Salcombe (see Differences SALCOMBE), whereas if it is at six in the morning or six in the evening, High Water at Salcombe is +10 minutes, or 10 minutes later.

If High Water Devonport is neither at 0100 or 0600 but, say 0330, then you must do a quick interpolation (by eye is usually sufficient) and decide that High Water Salcombe will be different by, in this case, +05 minutes. The same applies to the Differences for Low Water.

In the columns labelled 'Height (metres)' you will see the letters 'MHWS' etc. These mean quite simply 'Mean High Water Springs', and that if you have an average spring tide of 5.5m at Devonport, then the High Water at Salcombe will be 5.5m-0.2m, or 0.2 metres *less* and so on.

In practice, these simple calculations are less likely to come adrift if you write the information down systematically. Below is an example of how this might be done.

Left: The tidal information for Salcombe, from Macmillan's Nautical Almanac.

Note the following points:
- All times are in GMT and *Stated to be so.* If you always work in GMT you won't go wrong. Once you have the information 'boxed up' for Salcombe you can add an hour, if necessary, to work in BST.
- Time differences for HW Salcombe are interpolations. At 0600 the difference is +10 minutes. At 1300 the difference is zero. So in 7 hours it changes 10 minutes, which is about 1½ minutes per hour. Therefore at 1156, which is about one hour before 1300, the difference will be +1½ minutes. Half minutes are quite unrealistic when discussing tides, so you round up to the nearest whole minute and then apply your common sense to the situation.
- The range at Devonport shows that the tide is virtually a neap, so you do not need to interpolate between neap and spring height differences which, in this case, are negligable anyway.
- Because the tidal predictions are made on the basis of *astronomical* data, you cannot expect complete accuracy. The purity of astronomy is, unfortunately, interfered with by nasty, awkward intruders such as barometric pressure, sustained wind direction (maybe hundreds of miles away) and the like. So work your tides out as carefully as you can, and then allow a good margin for safety. That way you won't spoil your day and go away blaming the Hydrographer of the Navy.

Between high and low water

The soundings on the chart give you the depth above Chart Datum at the 'Lowest Astronomical Tide'. At almost any time the depth will be greater than this figure. The amount by which the actual depth exceeds the sounding on the chart is called the *height of tide*.

The tide tables offer you two heights of tide for a given period, those of High and Low Water. In practice you frequently want to know the height of tide at some time between those two figures.

Below: The times and heights of HW and LW at Salcombe on the morning of 16 July 1986.

	LW		HW		RANGE
	TIME	HEIGHT	TIME	HEIGHT	
PLYMOUTH (DEVONPORT)	0555 GMT	1.7m	1156 GMT	4.6m	2.9m
Differences SALCOMBE	−0005	−0.1m	+0002	−0.3	(Neap + a little)
SALCOMBE	0550 GMT	1.6m	1158 GMT	4.3m	2.7m

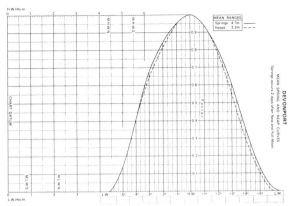

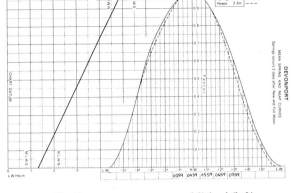

The Admiralty Tide Tables supply a simple, diagrammatic method of working this out and the necessary information is reprinted in Macmillan's and Reed's Almanacs. Each Standard Port has its own diagram which is presented alongside the tide tables.

In order to use the curve in the illustration, first look up the *heights* of High and Low Water and the *time* of High Water. Enter the time into the box (marked HW) beneath the curve and fill in the boxes in which you are likely to be interested to right or left of it. Take a ruler and draw a pencil line joining the values of LW (at the

Above: The Devonport curve as published (left), and as prepared for 23 February 1986 (above) using the information on times and tidal heights presented in the tide table (right).

Below: At what time, on 23 February 1986, will the tide have fallen to a height of 3.8 metres? Using the curve as prepared above, drop a construction line from the tide height scale at the top. From the point where it crosses the diagonal, move across to the 'tide falling' part of the curve, and plot vertically down to the time scale to give 0735 GMT.

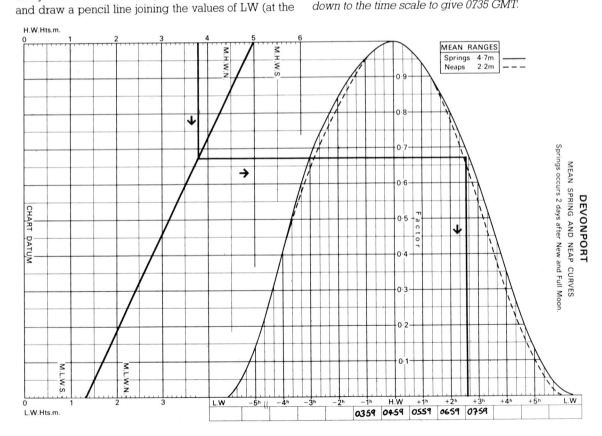

	TIME	M		TIME	M
1	0341	1.4	**16**	0353	1.8
	0932	5.2		0948	4.7
SA	1608	1.4	SU	1614	1.9
	2201	4.9		2218	4.5
2	0427	1.6	**17**	0434	2.1
	1019	5.0		1038	4.4
SU	1658	1.7	M	1700	2.2
	2255	4.7		2319	4.3
3	0525	1.8	**18**	0533	2.4
	1122	4.7		1150	4.1
M	1802	1.9	TU	1809	2.4
4	0008	4.5	**19**	0043	4.1
	0639	2.0		0704	2.5
TU	1248	4.5	W	1326	4.0
	1924	2.0		1951	2.5
5	0144	4.5	**20**	0214	4.2
	0812	2.0		0846	2.4
W	1435	4.5	TH	1453	4.1
	2052	1.9		2113	2.2
6	0316	4.7	**21**	0323	4.5
	0935	1.7		0948	2.0
TH	1559	4.6	F	1554	4.4
	2204	1.6		2206	1.9
7	0427	5.0	**22**	0415	4.7
	1040	1.3		1034	1.7
F	1704	4.9	SA	1641	4.7
	2303	1.3		2250	1.5
8	0527	5.3	**23**	0459	5.0
	1133	1.0		1115	1.3
SA	1759	5.1	SU	1725	5.0
	2352	1.0		2331	1.2

bottom of the left hand part of the diagram) and HW (at the top) for the tide in question. The diagram is now prepared.

The curves

You will notice that there are two curves very close to one another. One is depicted by a solid line and the other by a pecked line. At the top right-hand corner of the diagram there is a box showing the spring range with a solid line beside it, and the neap range with a pecked line. If the tide you are interested in has a range at, or close to the spring range you use the solid curve. If it is nearer the neap range, choose the pecked one. If it is halfway between, you should interpolate by eye between the two.

Secondary Ports

While the curves are prepared for Standard Ports, they also work for the related Secondary Ports. If you are concerned with a Secondary Port simply work out the

times and heights of High and Low Water (*at your port*) for the tide you want and apply them to the curve for the Standard Port.

The two big questions

There are two questions which the inshore navigator usually wants answered about tidal height. They are:
● At what time will there be a tidal height of so many metres?
● What will the tidal height be at a certain time?

What time?

As with all these workings you first join the High and Low Water heights for the day on the left of the diagram. Then you place your ruler vertically on the left-hand section at the required depth of water and draw a line downwards to cut the diagonal pencil line. Next you line your ruler up horizontally and join this point to the curve (either before, or after HW, as required) for spring or neap tides. Finally, you drop a vertical line from this point on

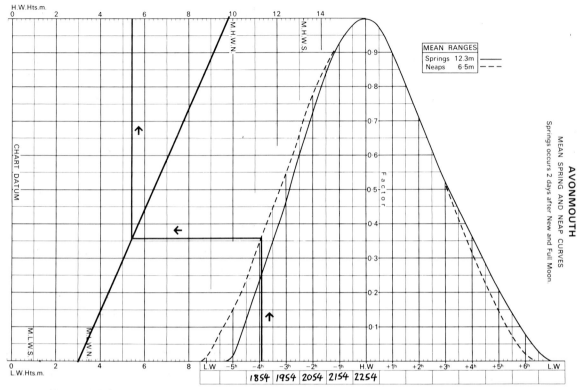

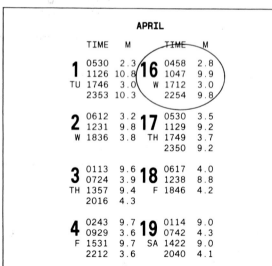

Left and above: What will the height of tide be at Avonmouth at 1900 GMT on 16 April 1986? Referring to the tide tables, fill in the time of HW in the time box, then fill in the adjacent boxes until you reach 1900 GMT. Draw in the diagonal line joining HW and LW, and note that it is virtually a neap range. Start the construction line at 1900 GMT, go to the neap curve, move across to the diagonal and up to the tide scale to get the answer: 5.4 metres.

How much water do you need?

When you are navigating in waters where the height of the tide decides whether or not your boat has enough water in which to float, you will often have to ask this question.

In general terms you should have some clearance under your keel. How much will depend on circumstances such as whether the tide is rising or falling, and the nature of the sea bottom, but as a general guide if you allow half your draft then you will not go far wrong.

the curve to your 'time boxes', and where it hits the base line is the time you are looking for.

How much water?

Calculations of *depth of water* at a *known time* work just the same as for the *time* of a *known depth*. You simply enter the diagram from the other end.

If your boat draws	1.50m
you may decide to allow	0.75m for clearance
meaning that you require	2.25m of water

Suppose Chart Datum for the place in question is 0_4 metres, then 0.4 metres of water is there all the time. You'll need an extra 1.85 metres (0.4 + 1.85 = 2.25) to give you as much water as you need. That extra 1.85 metres must come from the tide.

In this case if you were waiting to enter a very shallow harbour with a charted depth of 0.4 metres, the question you would need to ask the tidal curve diagram would be 'At what time will the height of tide have risen to 1.85 metres?'

And the answer is quite straightforward.

Drawing it

You may find it helpful to draw a small diagram here. It would look something like this:

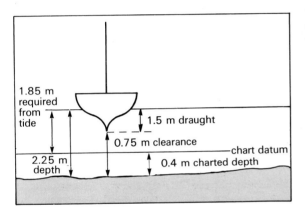

When you are approaching a harbour which dries out, you will certainly find a diagram helpful. If you are looking for your 2.25 metres of water, and your harbour dries 0.8 metres, your diagram will look like this:

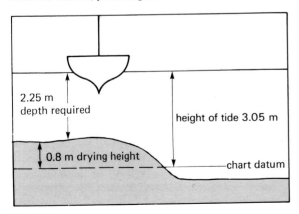

The height of tide required is 3.05 metres. At what time will the tide have risen to this figure? Go to the curve and find out.

Anchoring

An occasion when you want to know the depth at a specific time is when you are about to anchor. In this case you don't know exactly what the charted depth is, since you are probably anchoring between two soundings, or maybe up a creek where the soundings have petered out altogether.

The question you are asking here is this: 'I know what the *depth* of water is now from my echo sounder. From my tidal curve I know what the state of tide is. What will be the depth be at Low Water and, possibly, High Water?'

This one looks a bit tricky, but is actually the easiest of them all. From your tidal curve (duly 'filled in' for the tide in question), you work out how much the tide will fall from where you are now down to Low Water, and how much it will rise to High Water. By subtracting the amount it is going to fall from your current depth, you can see whether or not you'll be aground at Low Water.

If in doubt, draw a diagram. It will look like this:

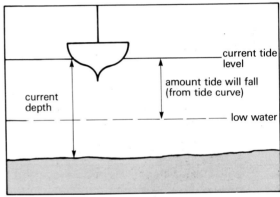

If you are going to anchor in the middle of a creek, always allow a bit of depth over and above the minimum because, when your boat swings with the tide, she may well embarrass you by swinging into shallower water.

The Solent and adjacent waters

Tides in the Solent area between Selsey Bill and Swanage behave quite eccentrically. This is as a result of the 'double High Water' caused by the presence of the Isle of Wight, and the effect is that the time of High Water is difficult to predict with any accuracy. Furthermore the tidal characteristics of the secondary ports in the area vary considerably.

For this reason, the secondary ports around the Solent are grouped together in various 'families', each of which has its own tidal curve. This is set out in the normal way, but it uses Low Water as its primary reference point in time rather than High Water. Otherwise the curves are used in exactly the same way as the curves for the remainder of the coastline.

Depth sounders

For thousands of years, seamen in search of the depth of water under them have laboriously dunked weights attached to long lines over the sides of their craft. This is inconvenient and very wet, but is reliable in still water or at slow speeds. It is next to useless at speeds over 4 knots and has long been hated by the foremast hands as a 'horror job'.

Since the 1940s the 'alternative leadline' has crept into use and now there is scarcely a decked vessel afloat that does not have an *echo sounder* as its primary means of measuring depth.

These instruments are cheap and very effective. The simple rotating L.E.D. (light emitting diode) type costs less than a week's dole money for an out-of-work leadline manufacturer, and will give years of reliable service.

It is possible to pay as much as you like for a sophisticated echo sounder, but for all inshore purposes the simpler it is, the better. Simpler also means cheaper, so in this case everyone is happy.

While it is possible to calibrate some of the more complicated instruments to read the depth under the keel, or the overall depth of the water, the usual small boat echo sounder reads only the depth below its own transducer. For this reason you need to remember two other measurements, or have them noted down in the back of your log book.

The first is the indicated depth at the moment you go aground. This is a most useful reading to know. It can be readily found by experiment (!) and once learned, is unlikely to be forgotten.

The second is the depth of the transducer below the surface of the water. It is important to know this one because most of your depth and tide calculations will be worked out for overall depth of the water. Your echo sounder will always 'under read' by its own depth below the surface and you will need to correct its readings to take account of this.

The leadline

All boats should have a leadline as a back-up, if for no other reason. A suitable lead weight can be bought from your local chandler (if he is worthy of the name) for the price of a round of drinks. Your line need not be very long because you will only use it for fine measurements of depth, such as you may require before taking the ground, or if you are anchored and it is touch and go whether you will float at Low Water. You can also take your leadline in the dinghy to 'sound out' your swinging circle when you are anchored.

In days of yore leadlines were marked with all manner of devices such as cloth, leather, bunting etc. so that the depth could be felt in the dark. Now that we have echo sounders that is no longer necessary. Some private code of your own is perfectly adequate, but in addition to whatever knots you may put in the line to mark the metres off, *do* put one at exactly the depth of your boat's draught. It doesn't take much imagination to see that it is the most important one of all!

Below: If you run aground, take the opportunity to check the depth of your echo sounder transducer above the keel of your boat. . .

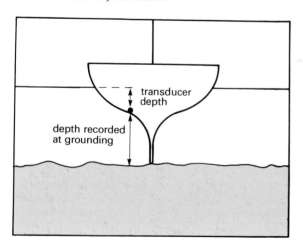

Below: The depth of the transducer below the surface of the water is added to the depth sounder reading to give the actual depth.

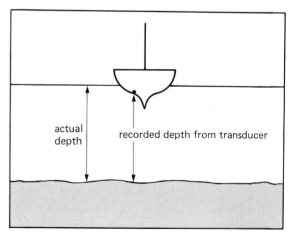

9 Fog

Fog is generally agreed to be one of the worst hazards you can meet at sea, so the first thing to do about it is avoid it if you can! Your local weather forecast will tell you if the day is likely to become foggy, and you can generally see for yourself when visibility is thicker than you feel able to handle.

However, because the likelihood of fog is sometimes difficult to pin down, then sooner or later you are going to get caught out – unless, of course, you become overcautious and that way you could miss a lot of good days on the water.

Fog is defined as any visibility less than one thousand metres. If you are navigating in a river or close to the shore a little fog may not bother you too much, but if you are out along the coast and the fog thickens up, you could lose sight of land and everything else as well. Even then things are not as bad as they seem. You still have a compass which you can, and must, trust. You have a log and you have an echo-sounder. Assuming you know where you were when you lost sight of your surroundings, or are able to work it out, then you are in a strong position.

The first thing to do, then, when you see visibility deteriorating, is to take as good a fix as you are able, and not to forget to log it. This is the rock on which all your navigational tactics will be built, so on no account miss your chance.

If for some reason you are unable to fix your position, then refer to your log entries and tidal information, and work up an Estimated Position as soon as possible.

Dangers

Fog in itself is not dangerous. It doesn't smell bad and it is entirely non-corrosive. It only causes trouble because it stops people seeing what is going on. Because of this the effect is greatly to increase the chances of two nasty occurrences.

The first of these is the danger of *collision*, and the second is the possibility of being *stranded* on the shore or on a reef that you have not been able to see.

In order to minimise both these dangers there are certain actions that you must take when you find yourself beset by fog. As we have said, the first priority is to fix your position, but as soon as that is done, you should make the following arrangements:

● *Hoist your radar reflector.* These devices come in two basic forms. Both should be hoisted as high as is convenient, if they are not permanently mounted. The radar reflector is your primary defence against being run down, because without it a big ship's radar is unlikely

Below: Two types of radar reflector: the traditional tetrahedron and the fully-enclosed 'Blipper'.

to see you until it is too late. It is the 'blip' of your reflector on her radar screen which is your salvation.

● *Look out and listen.* Because your circle of visibility is now so small you need all the look-out power you can get. The helmsman will be spending time peering at the compass, and will need at least one extra pair of eyes in the cockpit. If it's very thick, station someone on the foredeck as well. Remember he or she will see something a boat's length before you will, which just might save the day.

If you possibly can, *sail* rather than motor. Your ears are a vital piece of equipment now, and you need them to hear fog signals from buoys, lighthouses and ships. You may also hear breakers, a bow wave approaching, or even voices! Everything is important. If you have a motor running, turn it off every so often and listen. Your battery should be able to stand the extra 'starts' and the periodic silence might save your ship.

● *Make your own sound signal.* Your boat should carry a fog horn. The 'aerosol' type is a first-class option, but like all such devices the sea air has a way of snuffing them out. You should, therefore, carry a 'mouth-powered' horn as a back-up. These 'moose callers' can be surprisingly effective on the business end of a good pair of lungs.

If you are under power you should sound one long blast of about four seconds duration, at least once every two minutes. That's easy to remember, 'Here I come, sounding one'. If you hear another horn you can increase the frequency of your signals to ensure that you get your message across.

When sailing, you sound international code letter 'Delta', which is one long blast followed by two short ones. The same applies about frequency as when under power.

Sound signals and audible navigational aids such as bells and fog horns are a tremendous help, but you should always be aware that fog distorts sound waves. The fog signal you are hearing 30° on your starboard bow may really be almost abeam. Sound doesn't usually travel at all well upwind in fog, so if you are to windward of a signal you may not hear it until you are almost on it. Take great care with sound in fog.

Keeping out of the way

Of the two main dangers aggravated by fog, collision is by far the most likely, so your first priority is to avoid it at all costs. The worst type of collision is to be run down by a commercial vessel. If you are in a buoyed shipping channel when the visibility closes in, or if your fix shows you are somewhere near a likely shipping route, you should get clear of it as quickly as you can.

The safest course of action to avoid collision is to head for water that is too shallow for anything but vessels of your own draught or less. A few moments spent with the

Below: Using soundings to navigate to safe port in fog. Having taken a fix, head for the shore, then zig-zag along a reliable contour line until you reach the harbour entrance (see text).

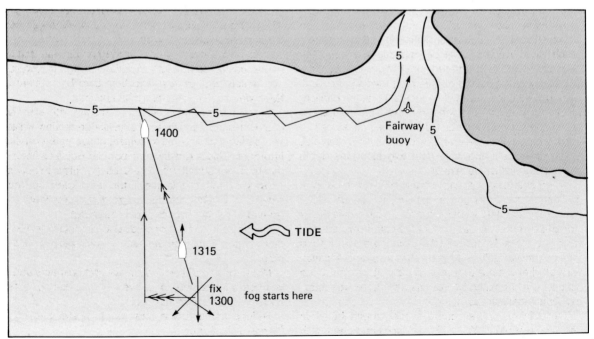

chart will show if there is a suitable spot to hide. You'll need to be discriminating in your choice, because the area needs to be sufficiently large for you to be unable to miss it. It should also be clear of navigational dangers and not have a strong wind blowing onshore. If your 'safe' area doesn't fulfil these requirements, then entering it may involve you in an unacceptable risk of the second danger, *stranding*.

The best way of avoiding both these possibilities is to find your way to a safe haven. As you sit out at sea in a hundred metres visibility this may seem an impossible task, but tackled coolly and logically it is often the best option.

The big secret

The one thing you do *not* do when approaching a harbour in fog is try to steer straight to the fairway buoy, or the pier head, or whatever the main entrance mark may be. Because of all the inbuilt possibilities for error in everybody's navigation, the chances of success would be slim indeed.

The first thing to do is to select a suitable harbour. This will be one where the coast on at least one side of the entrance is clear of all dangers for a reasonable distance, and has smooth but positive depth contours. It is surprising how many harbours fulfil this requirement. If there is a fog horn or a bell at the entrance, so much the better.

You then shape a course from your fix or EP so as to miss the entrance on the safe side by a good margin. How wide this margin is will depend on the circumstances, but it must be sufficient so that when you reach the shore you know beyond doubt whether the entrance lies on your port or your starboard hand.

While you are sailing or steaming towards the land, work out what the depth of water will be at the harbour mouth. As soon as you reach that depth it means that you are on the same contour as the entrance and, since you know which side of the entrance you are, it only remains to turn towards it and work your way along the depth contour to make a safe arrival.

When selecting a suitable contour line you need to find one where the bottom is shoaling at a steady rate. If the bottom is as flat as a billiard table for half a mile either side of the entrance mark, with only a couple of metres or so difference in depth for all that distance, you are going to have problems. The diagram shows an ideal situation with all the contours running clearly along the shore spaced quite positively. Fortunately, there are many harbours where this is the case.

There is one other pitfall to be careful of when choosing a contour. You will sometimes find one which

will leave you 'embayed' as illustrated below. It doesn't take much imagination to see that following a contour into a spot like this can lead to an ambiguous situation., Fortunately such kinks are rare, but be on the look-out for them all the same.

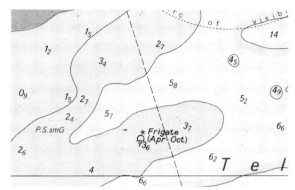

Above: Avoid choosing a contour that has tortuous curves in it – if you attempt to follow such a line in fog you will probably get lost.

If both sides of the harbour are equally suitable for an approach, choose the 'down-tide' coast. This is because you have more control when working up-tide since, for a given boat speed, your ground speed will be much lower.

The best technique to employ once you have turned onto your contour line is 40° *out*, 15°*in*. For example, if the shore is to port, steering 15° to port if the water deepens, and then making a 40° course alteration to starboard (i.e. 25° 'out' from the contour) as the water shoals to less than the desired depth, and so on.

This is an effective way of staying on the line. It also makes use of the natural inclination to edge in towards 'the beach' with caution, and then dive back towards deep water at the first smell of the bottom!

If you cannot find a suitable harbour with a useful contour to follow and there is no available shallow water, you have no choice but to remain at sea until visibility improves. This is usually an unpopular decision among thirsty crewmen but it is sometimes the only safe option. Hoist your radar reflector, listen, and keep up your navigation log, because the longer you are out there the greater are your chances of becoming lost.

Log any buoys, posts or otherwise identifiable objects that you see; it may be the last 'fix' you'll have for some time.

Make full use of any audible navigational aids and if you hear an 'unofficial' one, like a dog barking or a car horn, use your common sense!

Believe your compass, take your time and keep cool. It's only fog, after all.

10 The steering compass

For millenia seamen in Europe and the Middle East have been aware of the concepts of north, south, east and west. To the Ancients the north was the region whose direction was signified by the Pole Star. The east and west were defined by sunrise and sunset (and the Latin words for them mean literally that). The south was not quite so obvious in the days before the clock, but it was to be found in the direction of the sun at noon. Noon was not 'twelve o'clock' for Sinbad, it was the time when the sun reached its zenith and shadows were at their shortest.

No doubt the Chinese were there first, but for Western man the great breakthrough in navigation came sometime in the medieval period when an unknown mariner began to use a lodestone. He found that if he hung up this magnetised length of material by a string it would always align itself in a close approximation to north and south.

Accuracy was born and the road from there to the modern steering compass, if not always smooth, has at least been straightforward.

The compass is the most singleminded piece of equipment in a boat. It is attached to the fabric of the vessel and you have paid for it, but you cannot control its movements. As the Pole Star sits in silence over the axis of the planet, so the north pointer on your compass card resolutely indicates the direction of the magnetic North Pole, no matter what direction the boat is steering.

The boat turns, the compass does not. If you are out of sight of land under an overcast sky, or if you are in thick fog only a cable from the shore, your compass is your sole means of orientating yourself. Without it, you are lost.

Compass Deviation

Unfortunately the compass, in spite of its theoretical excellence as a navigating tool, is subject to forces which will create inaccuracies. In Chapter 1 we looked at Variation, which is the distance (expressed in degrees

Left: A steering compass mounted on the bulkhead.
Below: A pedestal compass.

west, or east) by which the magnetic north lies apart from the true north.

The compass roses on the chart give you all the information required to compensate for this, but there are other dark forces acting on your compass as well. These come from *within* the boat and can emanate from anything with enough iron in it, or enough of a magnetic field in its nature, to get a grip on the compass needle. The effect they produce is known as *Deviation*.

All sorts of items can cause Deviation. Some of them are permanently part of the boat, such as the engine. Others might be moveables like binoculars, fire extinguishers, torches, or even a stray screwdriver.

When you are using your handbearing compass you can generally take it to a part of the boat far enough away from these interferences for it to read accurately. A favourite spot in a fibreglass boat is close to the backstay which, as it is stainless steel, is not magnetically active.

You can't move a steering compass around like this because it must be mounted in a suitable place for the helmsman to be able to read it easily. You should therefore choose its location with care, and site it as far away from the engine (four feet – 1.2 metres – is the absolute minimum) as you can. Once the compass is sited make sure you stow all moveable magnetically-active materials as far away from it as is reasonably possible.

When the boat changes direction the compass card does not, so the attitude of the Deviation-producing items relative to the north pointer on the compass is going to alter with the ship's heading. However, so long as the compass and the lumps of iron remain in the same relative positions on the boat, the Deviation of the compass *on a given ship's heading* will always be the same. If it can be measured and noted down, the

Below: The compass is always pulled towards the engine, so Deviation changes with the heading.

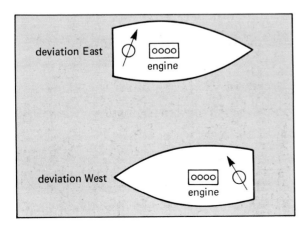

information will be available next time the boat is on that heading and the navigator can allow for it, thus removing the effect of the inaccuracy.

Because of the materials used in contemporary boat construction, it is not uncommon for a compass mounted in such a boat to have no Deviation at all. But in order to make sure where you stand, the best thing to do is to employ the services of a *compass adjuster*. He will carefully check the accuracy of your compass on a complete circuit of headings, and will do everything in his specialised power to eliminate any Deviation he may find. He does this by adjusting some tiny magnets built into most modern steering compasses, or by fixing compensating magnets to the ship in the vicinity of the compass if it doesn't have any. He is often able to reduce Deviation to the extent that it becomes an insignificant factor. Nevertheless if, when he has finished his work, there is still a measurable amount of Deviation remaining on some headings he will give you a *Deviation Card* which shows you what the error is on each of sixteen headings right round the compass.

Once you have a card, it is a good idea to plot it onto a graph, so that you can see at a glance what the Deviation is for any heading at all – not just the sixteen chosen by the compass adjuster.

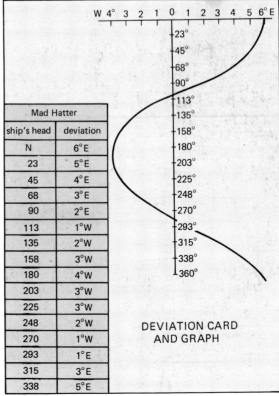

Mad Hatter	
ship's head	deviation
N	6°E
23	5°E
45	4°E
68	3°E
90	2°E
113	1°W
135	2°W
158	3°W
180	4°W
203	3°W
225	3°W
248	2°W
270	1°W
293	1°E
315	3°E
338	5°E

DEVIATION CARD
AND GRAPH

Swinging the compass

If you do not have a Deviation card, the simplest way to produce one is to find a quiet stretch of calm water, and then have one person standing by the backstay with the handbearing compass, while another steers the boat on each of the headings shown in the sample card illustrated. The difference, if any, in the readings of the two compasses is noted down and a Deviation card can then be produced.

If you have doubts about where to stand with the handbearing compass, you could tow your dinghy astern and do the job from there. You can sight very accurately on the boat's fore-and-aft line and, especially if the dinghy is an inflatable, you can be certain that the compass is not being interfered with. This method is a 'must' for steel boats, ferro-cement boats and wooden boats with iron fastenings, all of which are particularly subject to Deviation.

Applying Deviation

In the absence of Deviation, your steering compass reads in degrees Magnetic. What you have measured when you swung your compass and produced your Deviation card is how much your compass heading varies from that.

Just as in Chapter 1 we applied Variation to convert a *True* heading to a *Magnetic* heading, we are now applying Deviation to convert a *Magnetic* course to a *Compass* course.

The same rules apply about adding the value of the Deviation to, or subtracting it from, the Magnetic to convert it to the Compass, as applied for the conversion of True to Magnetic. You can use the same little

Below: Applying Deviation using diagrams.

diagrams to clarify the situation. Just as before,
ERROR WEST – COMPASS BEST
ERROR EAST – COMPASS LEAST

Example 1

During the compass swing you are steering 090°C on your ship's compass and the handbearing compass reads 095°M. What is the Deviation?

Clearly the Compass heading is *less* than the Magnetic heading: ERROR EAST – COMPASS LEAST. So the Deviation on a ship's head of 090°C is 5°E.

Example 2

Using the Deviation card on page 61, what is the compass heading you must steer to follow a course line measured at 180°M?

The Deviation on a heading of 180°M is 4°W. Since ERROR WEST – COMPASS BEST, you must add the Deviation, since the Compass heading is greater. So the Compass heading is 180 + 4 = 184°C.

You should bear in mind that Deviation on a particular heading is always measured from a Compass course rather than a Magnetic heading. If you are converting from Magnetic to Compass and you have a very large figure for the Deviation, this may give rise to a minor inaccuracy, but in nearly all circumstances the effects of this are negligible.

Course conversion

Since you will probably opt to work in Magnetic on the chart, most of the time, it will not be very often that you need to convert a Compass heading to a True heading. It will happen sometimes, though, and every now and again you'll need to convert from True right through to Compass as well.

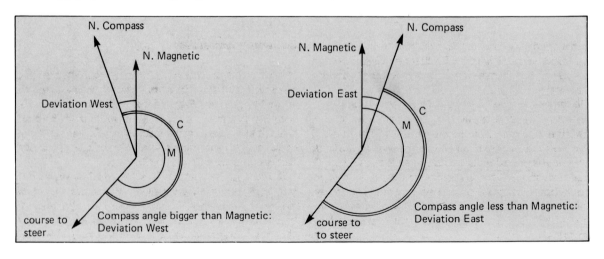

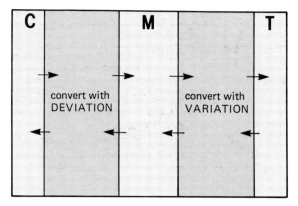

Above: Using the 'dual-carriageway' analogy to convert from Compass to True and back again.

Converting from True to Compass or vice versa is rather like crossing a dual carriageway with the Magnetic heading being the traffic island at which you stop in the middle.

Alternatively, to convert from Compass to True, simply remember the following:

Compass	:	**C**adbury's
apply **D**eviation	:	**D**airy
gives **M**agnetic	:	**M**ilk
apply **V**ariation	:	**V**ery
gives **T**rue	:	**T**asty

From True to Compass, simply remember:

True	:	**T**imid
apply **V**ariation	:	**V**irgins
gives **M**agnetic	:	**M**ake
apply **D**eviation	:	**D**ull
gives **C**ompass	:	**C**ompanions!

11 Conclusions

By studying the ten chapters in this book you have equipped yourself with all the theoretical knowledge you need to navigate a yacht safely along inshore seaways.

What you must do now is go out and 'get on with it' on the water. You understand the chartroom tools, how to use them and what information you should be drawing from the environment to be able to make them work for you, but only experience can turn you into a navigator. A year's seatime is worth a hundred books, and although the information you have been given has been presented from a highly practical point of view, it will only begin to slot into its true perspective as you log up the miles.

Accuracy and safety

Time will give you the experience to know what degree of accuracy to expect from your navigation in a given set of circumstances. Experience will teach you how accurate you need to be in your working at different times, but as always with the acquisition of new skills you begin with no experience at all. Therefore you should start out with the following philosophy.

Because of the inherent lack of precision in some of your input data, you cannot expect too much in the way of pin-point accuracy from your navigation. In consequence you should strive always to make your chartwork as neat and as careful as you can. In that way, at least, your efforts will not exacerbate any difficulties which circumstances beyond your control may have built into the situation.

Always allow a good margin for safety whenever it's possible to do so.

Confidence or over confidence?

It's an interesting commentary on human nature that very few people who think they may be lost come to any harm. The ones who 'come unstuck' are invariably convinced that they know where they are.

There is a natural tendency among navigators to make what we are actually seeing fit with what we know we really ought to be seeing. *Don't* ignore the faintest whiff of a rat. It is all too easy to discount that one buoy that 'doesn't quite fit in' with everything else you think you can see, and to assume that for some perfectly innocent reason it 'isn't on the chart'. Don't do it. Be honest with yourself and look the question squarely in the face. If one piece of the jigsaw just won't fit, then you may have forced a lot of others into place as well.

Remember there is no law against stopping to consider the situation. You can even turn round and go back the way you have come, and if you had enough depth of water to get this far, you should have enough to sail out again, unless the tide is dropping outrageously. Whatever you do, though, don't just plunge on when in doubt. Take your time, sort it out, and then proceed *positively* and in safety.

The skipper/navigator

On most yachts the skipper is the man who does the navigation. There are a lot of good reasons for this, not least among them being that navigation is one of the most satisfying elements of seafaring, and the skipper quite reasonably wants to hog it himself.

It is right and proper that the skipper should navigate his own boat but he must remember that knowing where he is, and steering in the right direction to arrive at his destination, is not an all-consuming pursuit and that it is only part of his job.

He also has to see that the boat is being properly sailed at all times. He must check the look-out and make decisions about potential collisions. He should do his share of steering and will often want to lead by example on the foredeck. If everyone on board including himself is feeling queasy, it is he who must tackle the ogre of the galley, and when his guest blocks the 'head' terminally, it is none other than the skipper who will find himself volunteering to strip it down.

If you are going to skipper your own boat the quicker and sharper your navigation is, the better, because the less time you spend on it, the more time you have for the rest of the business.

You wouldn't think of spending half an hour to make a cheese sandwich; well, taking a few bearings and plotting them on the chart should take about the same amount of time. Everyone is familiar with the loaf, the too-hard butter, the shrink-wrapped Cheddar soap substitute and the Blogston Pickle jar. If you practise with your navigation tools so that you achieve a similar familiarity, then navigation, pilotage and chartwork will soon become a simple, routine task.

Take your gear home and set yourself simple problems. Navigate the dining-room table to your favourite ports on winter evenings. Put your handbearing compass in the glove box of your car, and practise taking bearings quickly and accurately. But above all, *do go sailing.*

Think creatively about your navigation and in the early days each passage will provide a huge leap forward in your sifted experience. Spare ten minutes at the end of the day to run through what you have done, so as to consolidate your successes, and learn from your mistakes. You should make rapid progress and your own growing confidence will tell you when it is time to lengthen your stride and stand offshore towards the far horizon . . .